# PREPARING TO MANAGE

*Frameworks for Tenant Management Work Programmes and Competences for Tenant Management Organisations*

Suzie Scott
Keith Kintrea
Trish Ashworth
Janet Hale
Adrian Smith
Malcolm Williams

HMSO: LONDON

# Acknowledgements

This book was commissioned by the Department of the Environment as part of the guidance on the Right to Manage.

The work on frameworks for TMO work programmes was carried out by researchers at the University of Glasgow. The work on TMO competences was a collaboration between CDS (Liverpool) and the University of Glasgow. The support of these organisations is acknowledged.

Particular thanks are due to the 12 TMOs, who agreed to act as case-studies and pilots for the TMO competences and to the agency workers, local authority officers and specialists who provided information.

Helpful comments on drafts were received from the Tenant Participation Branch of the DoE, the project advisory group and participants at conferences and seminars where team members ran workshops.

The authors would also like to thank the people who assisted in the production of the book. Ann Rosengard carried out interviews for the frameworks for work programmes; Betty Johnstone typed the text and Hilary Parkey acted as proof-reader.

# Contents

**Acknowledgements**

**Chapter 1** **Introduction**

    About the Book
    The Right to Manage
    Feasibility Studies and Development Programmes
    Competence to Manage

**Chapter 2** **Feasibility Studies**

    Objectives
    Key Elements
    Time Inputs to Feasibility Studies
    Presentation of Feasibility Studies

**Chapter 3** **Development Programmes**

    Objectives
    Key Elements
    Time Inputs to Development Programmes
    Presentation of Development Programmes

**Chapter 4** **Competence to Manage**

    Introduction
    What is Competence?
    Existing Models
    What do TMOs Need to be Competent to do?
    Who Should be Competent?
    Who Should Assess Competence?

**Chapter 5** **Assessing Competence**

    Introduction
    Individual Abilities
    How Individual Competence Should be Assessed
    Group Competence
    Organisational Checklists
    Reporting on Competence

**Appendices**

1. Summary of Research Methods
2. Example Feasibility Programme
3. Example Development Programme
4. Feasibility Competences
5. Core Development Competences
6. Optional Development Competences
7. Organisational Checklist—Development
8. References

# Chapter 1   Introduction

**ABOUT THE BOOK**

This book is part of a series of books about the Right to Manage. It provides specific advice about the frameworks for the programmes of training and support which agencies and tenants receiving Section 16 funding must follow.

It also sets out guidelines for the assessment of competence of a TMO. It is aimed primarily at approved agencies, but it can also be used by tenants and local authorities.

The guidance is based on research which was carried out by the University of Glasgow and by TPAS (Scotland) on behalf of the Department of the Environment. The research report *Training for Tenant Management* set out typical programmes of activities followed by tenants who were developing TMOs and identified the key skills and knowledge required by TMOs at different stages of the process.

The research has been supplemented by further work to identify good practice, and a wide-ranging consultation process through interviews, correspondence and an advisory group. A summary of the aims and objectives of the projects, and the methods used, is included in Appendix 1. A list of other publications about the Right to Manage is given in Appendix 8.

**THE RIGHT TO MANAGE**

The Right to Manage allows tenants of local authorities in England and Wales to set up Tenant Management Organisations (TMOs). A TMO takes on a package of housing management responsibilities for a particular housing area or estate after entering into a management agreement with the local authority. Establishing a TMO means that a tenant-run body becomes responsible for some of the functions which were previously carried out by the local authority. A TMO has its own budget and, usually, its own staff.

In order to reach this position it is first required that the TMO should be a properly constituted body. The regulations require that organisations intending to consider the feasibility of a TMO must have an acceptable constitution, must be representative and accountable, serve a defined geographical area, and have a membership consisting of at least 20 per cent of tenants in the area. To make progress towards taking over management responsibilities the TMO must then serve a Right to Manage notice on the local authority. If this is valid, it triggers a programme of training and support for the TMO.

The Department of the Environment makes grants available to agencies and tenants' groups to assist in paying for the costs of advice, training and support. These grants are often called 'Section 16' grants, after the section of the Housing Act under which they are implemented.

All tenants' groups who want to exercise the Right to Manage with a view to setting up a TMO must appoint an agency from the Department's Approved List.

Approved agencies are responsible for:

- setting up work programmes
- identifying what tenants need to learn
- arranging training
- assessing the competence of the TMO
- drawing up the Management Agreement
- keeping residents and the local authority informed

**FEASIBILITY STUDIES AND DEVELOPMENT PROGRAMMES**

There are two main parts of the programme of training and support for TMOs. The first is a TMO feasibility study, which is intended to explore the possibility of increasing tenants' influence in the management of their estate. If this shows that a successful TMO is feasible, a TMO development programme can begin. The development programme is intended to provide the support and training necessary for the TMO to take over the management of its estate successfully. The Right to Manage Regulations issued by the Department of the Environment refer to the feasibility study as the *initial feasibility study* and the development programme as the *full feasibility study*. This book refers to 'feasibility studies' and 'development programmes' throughout.

The main activities during feasibility studies and development programmes should be based on the common frameworks outlined in this book. The frameworks are designed to ensure that all TMOs are established on the basis of a full exploration of the options for management and that the TMO's committee receives adequate training for the range of management functions being devolved by the local authority.

The purpose is not to impose a strict and inflexible agenda, but to provide a framework for tenants and agencies around which feasibility studies and development programmes can be constructed.

The guidance on these frameworks has three components:

- The first outlines the content of feasibility studies and development programmes which is distilled into sets of key elements.
- The second suggests the proportion of time which might be spent by agencies on each of these elements.
- The third component is guidance on the presentation of the programmes of work.

**Content**

For each of the stages of feasibility and development a set of key elements is laid out. These are summarised in Tables 1 and 2, and discussed in full in Chapters 2 and 3. The core elements reflect the guidance on training suggested in *Learning to Manage* and requirements for competence.

These elements consist of training activities, but also:

- administrative activities
- communication activities

- policy development
- decision-making
- negotiation activities
- monitoring and review.

**Proportion of Time**

The key elements must form the basis of all feasibility studies and development programmes. However, the frameworks recognise that the experience and expectations of TMOs are very varied, and the material and social conditions of housing areas differ markedly from place to place. This means that the overall attention to each element is likely to vary between different TMOs, and within each element there is scope for some variation in the activities actually undertaken. Guidance on time inputs is given at the end of Chapters 2 and 3.

**Presentation**

It is important that the work programmes are presented in a way which makes the components explicit. Example feasibility and development programmes are shown in Appendices 2 and 3.

**COMPETENCE TO MANAGE**

Under the Right to Manage legislation, properly constituted local authority tenants' organisations have a right to take over the management of their homes. However, local authorities have discretion to refuse to enter into an agreement if they have grounds for believing that a prospective TMO is not competent to manage.

It would be manifestly unjust if tenants in different parts of the country, and assisted by different agencies, were assessed in different ways. In order to ensure that similar criteria are applied, the Department of the Environment commissioned a study to draw up a recognised set of baseline competences that could be understood and applied by prospective TMOs, agencies and local authorities.

Chapter 4 of this book outlines what competence is, what TMOs need to be competent to do, who should be competent and who should assess competence.

The assessment of competence is a three-part process which encompasses:

- individual abilities
- group competence
- organisational policies and procedures.

Chapter 5 describes how competence can be assessed.

**Competence at the Feasibility Stage**

At the feasibility stage tenants need to have the ability to carry out the tasks involved in the work programme and prepare for the development stage. These will be developed through training and practical activities. The TMO should also show that the tenants' organisation is acting in accordance with its constitution and has adequate committee, administration and financial procedures. The feasibility competences are given in Appendix 4.

**Competence at the Development Stage**

At the development stage, the tenants must make a number of choices about the responsibilities they wish to take on. The range and level of responsibilities chosen will vary from TMO to TMO. The level of competence required must also be flexible. However, all TMOs need certain 'core' abilities which are concerned with managing the organisation. The individual competences, at the development stage, are divided into 'core' and 'optional' abilities and are included in Appendices 5 and 6.

Finally, during the process of negotiating the management agreement, the prospective TMO should have developed appropriate policies and procedures for the functions it will take responsibility for. Systems for financial control and tenant involvement should also have been developed. The organisational competence can be assessed through scrutiny of these systems. A checklist of the policies and procedures which should be in place by the time that the agency produces the development report is given in Appendix 7.

**Competence at Handover**

Once a satisfactory development report has been submitted and accepted, and a favourable ballot held, the TMO must establish its office, finalise systems and employ staff. This work is not included in the TMO competences but a checklist of organisational systems is given for guidance in *The Guide to the Right to Manage*.

# Chapter 2  Feasibility Studies

**OBJECTIVES**

The objective of a feasibility study is to explore the possibility of increasing tenants' involvement in the management of their estate. The focus is on the potential to establish a TMO. The feasibility study should aim to examine the available options for extending tenant participation and maximise the involvement of all residents in making decisions about management in the future. It should also equip the tenants' group with some of the skills and knowledge they need in order to take on a management role.

Its duration is likely to be between three months (in exceptional cases, if the tenants' committee or board is already well-established and the estate is small) to nine months at the very longest (if the committee is inexperienced, and the estate is large and its problems complex). Six months is likely to be the average.

The programme of the feasibility study in part consists of training events for the committee members of the TMO examining options for the estate's future management. It is also an investigation into the support for tenant involvement among local people and the housing problems of the estate and other issues which are causing concern among residents. The feasibility programme then, must incorporate training activities, consultation and liaison, and some research.

The content of feasibility studies comprises 12 main elements which are essential to a successful programme. These should form the framework around which bids for Section 16 funding are built. As far as possible all the activities of the feasibility study should fall within these elements, and all 12 elements should normally form part of every feasibility study. While there is an obvious sequence to many of the elements, some may usefully run in parallel and this is noted where appropriate. In particular, the elements of Communication and Monitoring and Review should feature regularly throughout the programme.

**KEY ELEMENTS**
**1. Planning the Feasibility Study**

After selecting a suitable agency, the first stage for the tenants' group is to agree the detailed content of the feasibility study, and to plan its meetings and activities. This element of the work needs to be undertaken before anything else takes place. The elements which usually require most careful planning are Assessing the Estate's Problems and Priorities and Assessing the Support for Resident Involvement.

The draft programme needs to be drawn up by the agency and agreed with the committee. The committee must agree upon its own role and responsibilities with respect to the implementation of the programme. Tenants will need to have early training on feasibility studies and what to expect out of them, and should undertake a session examining their own training needs. These needs should be reflected in the programme of the feasibility study.

At the planning stage, liaison with the local authority's officers needs to be undertaken in order to agree and plan the council's input (if any) to the feasibility study. *Learning to Manage* recommends that the council takes part in training sessions. In addition, tenants' organisations may request 'reasonable' training and support from the local authority to help them progress the TMO.

Knowledge of the existence and purpose of the feasibility study must also be promoted among the majority of residents who are not involved in the committee. This might be done by a combination of door-to-door contact, public meetings, and a newsletter or circular.

*Table 1* Key elements of feasibility studies

| | | |
|---|---|---|
| 1. | Planning the Feasibility Study | Meetings to agree the feasibility study and plan its activities |
| 2. | Assessing the Estate's Problems and Priorities | Data collection, surveys and meetings to collect information about the estate |
| 3. | Assessing the Support for Tenant Involvement | Activities to gauge the level of support among tenants for tenant management |
| 4. | Exploring Management Options | Training on TMOs and their alternatives |
| 5. | Understanding Housing Management and Finance | Basic training on local authority management and functions |
| 6. | Preparing for a Management Role | Training in the skills needed to lead and represent the community |
| 7. | Assessing Competence | Assessing the competence of the tenants' group |
| 8. | The Feasibility Report | Drafting, validating and finalising the report |
| 9. | The 'Test of Opinion' | A ballot or poll of all tenants on their support for a TMO |
| 10. | Planning for the Development Stage | Training and agreement on the development stage |
| 11. | Communication | Communication with local residents and the local authority |
| 12. | Monitoring | Monitoring progress of the programme and of the group |

## 2. Assessing the Estate's Problems and Priorities

The training agency must undertake an extensive review of the estate in order to determine the range and extent of its physical and social problems. In larger estates, in particular, this element is likely to be the single greatest part of the feasibility study. This activity can go on in parallel to training designed to help tenants consider the options that are available (see Exploring Management Options below).

The estate assessment should involve collation of any available data and reports relating to the estate, discussions with relevant agencies, council departments and elected members. Views of residents at large should be sought through open meetings, discussion groups or role playing, for example. More intensive door-to-door, or block or street surveys may be useful according to individual circumstances. These may illuminate more clearly key areas of concern, e.g. a door-to-door survey about repair services; a traffic or parking survey.

Each estate assessment should be carried out with reference to a checklist of key items, but the agency should ensure that the agenda reflects the concerns of the tenants. At a minimum it should cover the items in Table 2.

The estate assessment should clearly identify those shortcomings which could be addressed by establishing a TMO and those which would require other kinds of action.

Emerging findings need to be reviewed with the TMO's committee before being crystallised. Estate problems which are outside the scope of a TMO to tackle need to be discussed with the local authority and other relevant agencies with a view to building an overall strategy for the estate.

*Table 2* Feasibility study: estate assessment

*Housing Conditions*
Major physical shortcomings with the existing housing stock, for example disrepair, dampness, design defects, amenity deficiencies, mismatch of stock characteristics with housing needs.

*Housing Management*
For example voids, rent arrears, caretaking, tenancy management problems, repairs systems.

*Physical Environment*
Deficiencies in the estate's environment, e.g. disrepair, road layout and parking, pedestrian safety, access routes, cleanliness and upkeep.

*Amenities*
Amenities and commercial facilities in the estate, transport links and relative location.

*Social Conditions*
Household types and ages, any social divisions within the estate, the make-up of the community including ethnic mix, crime, and fear of crime.

*Economic Conditions*
Employment and unemployment.

**3. Assessing the Support for Resident Involvement**

The feasibility study must take stock of the level and nature of support that exists among residents of the estate as a whole for a greater degree of tenant involvement. For a TMO to succeed it needs to develop a high level of support from residents, and be representative of the various groups and opinions that exist locally. The programme needs to include means of creating a dialogue with the majority of residents who are not involved in the committee or board. These might include door-to-door surveys, exhibitions, open days or public meetings. The object is to outline in a balanced way the opportunities for tenant involvement and the options being considered in the feasibility study. This element of the feasibility work may be combined, if appropriate, with the assessment of estate problems and solutions.

**4. Exploring Management Options**

The committee needs to get specific training on the range of options available to increase tenant influence in housing management. Service of the Right to Manage notice prior to the feasibility study may imply in many cases that a fully-functioning TMO is preferred. Even where this is clearly the case, the feasibility study must consider whether this really is the preferred option for the estate. At this point training should concentrate on the broad structures of the alternatives, and should promote an understanding of the role and responsibilities of tenants within each option. The advantages and disadvantages of each model should be considered, together with the implications for rents and rent-setting, tenancy rights and capital investment opportunities.

Three main types of option should be explicitly examined:

i) **tenant participation or consultation options**:— more limited lower-level options including tenants' liaison committees, estate sub-committees etc, designed to increase tenants' influence on council management without changes in formal responsibilities. Many tenants' groups will be already working within well-developed participation structures. It should be noted that all councils will be putting in place arrangements to involve tenants in specifying levels of service in preparation for competitive tendering of housing management

ii) **tenant management options**:— a tenant management organisation, with extent and level of responsibility to be established using the Modular Management Agreement

iii) **transferred ownership options**:— transfer of ownership of the housing to a housing association or ownership co-operative, either by voluntary transfer or Tenants' Choice.

In addition to these a 'business as usual' option needs to be considered, although in nearly all cases this is likely to be unacceptable.

Examination of these options can take place by means of in-house training, and by visits to existing schemes which have faced similar problems. The programme of meetings must ensure that an eventual choice between these options is made in the full knowledge of the advantages and disadvantages of each in relation to the problems and opportunities presented in the housing estate.

## 5. Understanding Housing Management and Finance

The fifth key element of the programme is for the committee to achieve a basic understanding of how the council works, in preparation for discussions about the possible take-over of some existing council functions. At this stage the training needs to be of sufficient depth to promote a general understanding of structures and functions. Detailed consideration of policies and procedures can be left until the development programme.

Training should include material on the housing management responsibilities of local authorities (including legal duties, housing management functions, organisation, roles of officers and members, CCT and the Right to Manage) and on housing finance (including capital and revenue budgets and rent-setting). If appropriate, an understanding of other elements of council service to the estate needs to be promoted.

## 6. Preparing for a Management Role

The feasibility study must include training for the committee in the skills and approach that its members need in order to lead the community, to represent it to the council, and to negotiate the best deal for its tenants. This element of the feasibility programme embraces key training topics on: representing the community; equal opportunities; working as a group; and negotiation skills.

## 7. Assessing Competence

The feasibility study must ensure that the progress of the tenants' group, at the core of the TMO, towards competence is monitored. In this respect, particular responsibility lies with the support agency. If it seems unlikely that the proposal for tenant management is going to succeed, for example because of widespread popular opposition to tenant management, or a failure of the TMO's committee, the Department of the Environment requires the feasibility study to be curtailed before its planned completion date. Similarly, there is a requirement for the support agency to conclude the feasibility study if the committee of the TMO is not acting in accordance with its constitution, or is not reasonably representative, or is motivated to pursue tenant management in order to exclude some sections of the estate's residents.

## 8. The Feasibility Report

The main output of the feasibility study is the feasibility report. It is the responsibility of the training agency to produce this report, initially in draft, then to finalise it after consultation with the committee and with the council. The feasibility report, at minimum, should include the sections listed in Table 3.

*Table 3* The feasibility report

1. *Introduction*
   - previous promotion work and results
   - why the study is being undertaken

2. *The Feasibility Study*
   - objectives
   - work programme
   - training undertaken
   - tenants' views on training

3. *The Estate, including*
   - number and type of dwellings
   - housing conditions
   - housing management
   - physical environment
   - amenities
   - social conditions
   - economic conditions

4. *The TMO's Competence*
   - individual competence
   - group competence
   - organisational competence

5. *Relationship with the Local Authority*

6. *Local Authority Management Structures*

7. *Options for Tenant Involvement Examined*
   - methods of consultation
   - feedback on options, including any survey results
   - the chosen option and why it is preferred
   - viability of the chosen option
   - if a TMO, functions to be delegated

8. *Any Concerns or Unresolved Problems*
   - problems that are outside the scope of a TMO

9. *Conclusion and Recommendations*

Copies of newsletters, minutes of meetings etc, should also be attached as appendices

## 9. The 'Test of Opinion'

Testing the opinion of residents is the ultimate phase of assessing demand for resident involvement at the feasibility stage. A test of opinion should only be carried out after the training agency has filed a positive feasibility report on the TMO. The report must indicate that the potential to develop a fully-operational TMO exists, and that the TMO is operating properly within its constitution, and is reasonably representative of people in the area.

The TMO can only be taken forward to the development stage if a majority of tenants (including a majority of secure tenants) taking part in a poll or ballot say they are in favour. Tenants can vote by means of a door-to-door survey or ballot, or a poll or ballot using polling stations. The council will make the arrangements for the poll or ballot, in consultation with the agency and the TMO.

Whichever method is chosen, it is up to the committee and its agency to encourage the maximum turnout for the vote.

## 10. Planning for the Development Stage

If a majority of tenants voting in the ballot support the TMO, the development phase must start within six months. This means that the conclusion of the feasibility study must anticipate the start of the development programme. The committee of the TMO should receive training on what a development programme is, on recruitment practice and interviewing skills to enable selection of a suitable development agent, and on identifying what the group's future training needs are.

The final element of the feasibility programme is for the training agency to produce an initial outline of the development programme for the forthcoming application by the TMO for Section 16 funding for the development stage. More liaison with the council's staff and members is also necessary at this final stage.

## 11. Communication

Communication is a vital activity at the feasibility stage. In order for a successful TMO to be developed, the committee and its agency must communicate regularly with the key groups. These are the wider community within the estate who are not involved in the committee or board, and the local council. Regular communication, then, should feature as an explicit component of the feasibility study.

A TMO puts housing management into the collective control of tenants. So, in order for any proposal to develop a TMO to be successful, there is a need to carry uninvolved residents in the area along with the committee. A specific element of the programme for the feasibility study should be regular newsletters or circulars to inform residents about the options being considered, and to encourage them to become involved. Communication should also take place with residents through formal and less formal open meetings.

Regular communication with local authority officers and local elected members should also feature as an explicit part of the programme. This is important whether or not the local authority is supportive of the Right to Manage and whether or not a proposal for a TMO emerges from the feasibility study. If a TMO is in prospect, the committee will be looking for funding from the local authority at the development stage and to negotiate a management agreement. If it is not, the committee will probably want to explore means of increasing resident involvement within existing structures. Either way, the council's support will help the proposal to succeed.

## 12. Monitoring

Monitoring is a necessary activity for both main parties involved in the feasibility study. In addition to monitoring of competences discussed earlier, there are three other key aspects of monitoring. First, it is necessary for the agency and the tenants' group together to monitor the overall progress of the programme. It is an inevitable feature of progressing towards a TMO that there will be uncertainty. It is likely that the timetable of activities planned for the feasibility study at the outset will need adjustment to accommodate unexpected events or opportunities. The programme needs to be reviewed while it is being carried out to ensure that the key elements remain in place and can be accommodated within the programme.

Second, the agency's work in delivering the feasibility study should be monitored by the committee. The committee should try to ensure that the agency is providing all the inputs agreed in the programme, and that the quality of its work is acceptable. Training sessions should always incorporate an opportunity for tenants to produce feedback on the quality of the training received.

Third, the progress of feasibility studies must be reported to the Department of the Environment which funds the studies. The DoE requires quarterly financial reports and six-monthly progress reports to be submitted by the training agency, and these should be built into the programme.

All of this means that monitoring needs to be incorporated in the programme as a specified activity at regular intervals, in case there is a need to adjust the programme, reconsider the TMO's needs or to abort the work. There is likely to be value in involving the local authority in assisting with monitoring, providing that all parties are agreeable, and the local authority's role is clearly defined.

**TIME INPUTS TO FEASIBILITY STUDIES**

Adequate time must be devoted to each of the key components of feasibility studies. While the tenants' committee's time is unpriced, the agency's time input must be specified in the bid for funding to carry out the work programme. The time available to be spent on the programme by the agency depends on three factors: the size of the estate (which drives the Department of the Environment's formula for the maximum allowable expenditure); the time devoted to travelling as a proportion of the total input, and the hourly rate of the agency. These factors mean that there can be considerable variation between the time available for preparation and delivery of the programmes.

In spite of this variety, there is little point in providing a framework for the content of the work programme without also giving some guidance on the necessary time input for each of the essential components. Table 4 lays out suggested minimum and maximum proportions of time (including travel, preparation and meeting time) to be spent on each of the key components of feasibility studies. Normally, the time the agency devotes to each component in the feasibility study should fall between these limits. The principle is illustrated by a 300 hour programme for a feasibility study.

**PRESENTATION OF FEASIBILITY STUDIES**

Appendix 2 provides an example of how a work programme should be laid out in the application for Section 16 grant. This style of presentation is designed to make the components of the programme and their incidence over time explicit. It provides an easily-readable overview of the programme which can be used for planning and monitoring purposes by tenants, agencies, and the Department of the Environment.

The activities shown in the programme are not intended to be definitive—the detailed content of the programme will be planned according to the needs of the tenants and their estate.

Feasibility programmes, because of their short time span, need to be expressed in full detail from the outset. Proposed input hours by the agency can be added to each column and row to aid assessment and monitoring of programmes.

*Table 4* Feasibility studies: suggested minimum and maximum time inputs
Example based on a 300 hour programme for an estate of about 300 dwellings

| Component | Minimum Hours | % of Time | Maximum Hours | % of Time | Average Hours | % of Time |
|---|---|---|---|---|---|---|
| 1. Planning the Feasibility Study | 5 | **2** | 15 | **5** | 9 | **3** |
| 2. Assessing the Estate's Problems | 60 | **20** | 90 | **30** | 75 | **25** |
| 3. Assessing Support for Tenant Involvement | 45 | **15** | 60 | **20** | 51 | **17** |
| 4. Exploring Management Options | 36 | **12** | 60 | **20** | 48 | **16** |
| 5. Understanding Housing Management and Finance | 20 | **7** | 36 | **12** | 28 | **9** |
| 6. Preparing for a Management Role | 20 | **7** | 36 | **12** | 28 | **9** |
| 7. Assessing Competence | 5 | **2** | 8 | **3** | 6 | **2** |
| 8. The Feasibility Report | 9 | **3** | 15 | **5** | 12 | **4** |
| 9. The 'Test of Opinion' | 9 | **3** | 30 | **10** | 18 | **6** |
| 10. Planning for the Development Stage | 6 | **2** | 15 | **5** | 9 | **3** |
| 11. Communication | 6 | **2** | 15 | **5** | 9 | **3** |
| 12. Monitoring | 4 | **1** | 10 | **3** | 7 | **2** |
| Total | 225 | **75** | 390 | **130** | 300 | **100** |

Note: Percentages have been rounded where necessary

# Chapter 3  Development Programmes

**OBJECTIVES**

The development stage of a TMO is intended to take the positive support evident at the end of the feasibility study forward to the establishment of a fully-functioning TMO. Its main aim is to create a competent TMO — one whose management committee has the skills and knowledge required to run a housing organisation. This means that the committee should be up to the task of carrying out the functions which are delegated by the local authority under the Right to Manage. The management functions should be appropriate to local people's requirements and demands.

Development programmes incorporate a significant training element. This is intended to develop a clear idea of the range of functions to be taken on by the TMO and to prepare the committee for negotiating the management agreement with the local authority. Training is also required for carrying out the management responsibilities that the TMO will shoulder after it becomes fully operational. This involves training in both knowledge of good housing practice and in the skills of management.

As well as training, the development stage also involves administrative work, outreach work within the community, communication with the local authority, and a significant monitoring role for the training agency.

A development programme can last up to two years. The content of the development programme can be divided into 13 main elements. These apply whatever the range of management functions to be taken over by the TMO. Within items 3, 5 and 6 (below) the content of the programme will vary according to the option being pursued.

*Table 5*  Key elements of development programmes

| | | |
|---|---|---|
| 1. | Planning the Development Programme | Meetings to agree the development programme and its activities |
| 2. | Agreeing the TMO Group's Structure and Responsibilities | Training and decision making on the role of the TMO committee and the distribution of responsibilities during the development programme |
| 3. | Incorporating the TMO | Legal registration of the TMO as an Industrial and Provident Society or a company limited by guarantee, or limited by shares |
| 4. | Introducing the Modular Management Agreement | Training on available choices of management functions and levels of responsibility |
| 5. | Working up the Management Options | Training, decision-making and policy development about the desired management options |
| 6. | Preparing to Run a Housing Organisation | Training in management skills |
| 7. | Negotiating the Management Agreement | Training in, and carrying out negotiations with the local authority |
| 8. | Assessing Competence | Assessing the competence of the TMO |
| 9. | The Development Programme Report | Completion by the agency of the report outlining the proposals for the TMO, and its competence |

| | | |
|---|---|---|
| 10. | Assessing Tenants' Support | A continuous programme of outreach activities among uninvolved tenants, culminating in the ballot |
| 11. | Setting up the TMO | Signing the agreement and setting up the new organisation |
| 12. | Communication | Communication with local residents and the council |
| 13. | Monitoring | Monitoring the progress of the programme and the group |

**KEY ELEMENTS**
**1. Planning the Development Programme**

Following the selection of a training agency for the development stage, the TMO's first activity is to agree the detailed content of the development programme, and to plan its meetings and activities. The development programme must reflect the TMO's own views of its training needs and priorities, and the decisions that have been made in principle at the feasibility stage about the desired functions to be managed by the TMO. However, the training programme must also ensure that the group is going to progress towards full competence as a TMO, and it is the agency's responsibility to ensure that the programme will achieve this. Agreeing and planning the work programme must be undertaken before anything else takes place.

An initial idea of the development programme will have been formed in the concluding stage of the feasibility programme. A full draft programme now needs to be drawn up by the training agency, and the costings and the programme agreed with the committee of the TMO.

Because of the length of the development programme and the inevitable uncertainty about its negotiation phase, it is not necessary to plan every single meeting or activity in advance. The first six month's programme should be given in detail and the second six month's broadly sketched out. The plan for the second year of the programme needs only to indicate the broad division of time between the key elements of the programme, and their desired sequence.

The implementation of the development programme needs to be worked out, and the division of responsibilities planned between the committee, the lead support agency, and any sub-contractors. (Sub-contractors may be brought in to fulfil specialist training or support needs that the lead agency will not deliver by using its own staff.)

It is also likely that the local authority will want to play a role in the development programme by providing training, or by providing material or financial support for the TMO over and above its contribution to the cost of the agency's input. The local authority is obliged to comply with reasonable requests made by the TMO for help at this stage. This means that time must be built into the planning element of the programme to accommodate the necessary liaison with the council's staff and/or members.

**2. Agreeing the TMO Group's Structure and Responsibilities**

Early decisions need to be made on how the committee will operate during the development phase, and time for training and agreement on this needs to be built into the programme. Until this point the group may have acted relatively informally, but now it must begin to prepare itself for the serious business of taking over the management of the estate.

The committee must consider and establish its structure and its procedures for management, including any sub-groups, and its schedule of meetings. In some cases a clear distinction will need to be made between the TMO and the original tenants' group which spawned it, which might continue in existence. It must decide where responsibility lies for executive action and implementation of decisions, and for liaison with key individuals and groups, including the Department of the Environment, the agency and the local authority. To reach this position, most TMOs will need training, or at least a structured presentation of the options for management that are available.

Following this, the development programme should address the role and responsibilities of the committee's office-bearers. The usual officers would be Chairperson, Secretary and Treasurer. These will usually be in place but their roles are enhanced as responsibility increases. The tenant's organisation needs to agree and define these positions following training; the individuals holding the posts are likely to require further training to develop their competence in the tasks agreed to be their responsibility.

## 3. Incorporating the TMO

In order to enter into a management agreement with the local authority, the TMO must become incorporated by registering with an appropriate body. The development programme must then take the organisation to registration as an Industrial and Provident Society, a company limited by guarantee, or a company limited by shares.

The lead-up to this decision needs training for the committee on the implications of the models and some time must be allowed to prepare documentation, and correspond with the registration body.

Establishing a formal organisation raises questions about the wider membership of the TMO. The development programme should build in efforts to encourage tenants to become shareholders in the new organisation, which gives them a right to be involved in election to the committee. Encouragement could take the form of door-to-door canvassing, and application forms to join the TMO could be included in newsletters.

Finally under this heading, consideration needs to be given to whether, and if so how, the membership of the committee needs to be strengthened in terms of its numbers, representativeness and skills. A committee which has served well at the feasibility stage may now need additional members to ensure wider representation and to avoid the burden of office falling too heavily on a few people. If new people join, allowance has to be made in the programme for training to bring them up to speed with the rest of the group.

## 4. Introducing the Modular Management Agreement

The device which will structure the relationship between the future TMO and the local authority is the Modular Management Agreement. This sets out the choices which can be made about the management functions the TMO can take over from the council. It also offers choices about the level of responsibility. The development programme must include training for the committee on the structure of the Modular Management Agreement, its main choices (modules), and its negotiation and implementation.

Because the TMO will be taking over some of the local authority's functions it is essential that the tenants fully understand how the council operates its housing service. Consideration of the Modular Management Agreement needs to be backed up by training on local authority structures and management, and on housing finance. This training should address specifically the structures and practices of the TMO's local authority. The training should build upon earlier and more general training during the feasibility study, and promote an understanding of how the TMO will engage with existing local authority structures and procedures, and consider how the TMO will be financed.

## 5. Working up the Management Options

The TMO will be looking to take over a range of functions from the local authority. These will vary significantly between different TMOs. The functions could include maintenance and repairs, rent collection and arrears recovery, housing allocations, tenancy management and estate caretaking. The development programme should focus on each function in turn. The committee must decide whether or not to take on the function, and what degree of control they are looking for. The development programme should then focus on providing the skills and knowledge required by the committee to make policy on these functions, and to carry them out. So the development programme here needs to be a combination of training, policy development and decision-making. In addition, it could be useful for committee members to meet with the local authority staff in order to explore areas of concern in implementing tenant management.

The programme of training activities needs to be geared primarily to the functions envisaged to be carried out by the TMO. However, it will be necessary to undertake less intensive training on issues which lie outside the TMO's immediate responsibilities. This is for two reasons. First, it is likely that the TMO office will be the first point of call for tenants regardless of whether their enquiry is connected with a function taken over by the TMO, or one which remains with the council. Second, many functions taken over by the TMO will still leave the council with some responsibilities, for example legal action on rent arrears may remain with the council, even if the main responsibilities for rent collection and arrears control lies with the TMO.

## 6. Preparing to Run a Housing Organisation

It takes more to run a housing organisation than technical knowledge of allocation policies, repairs procedures and other housing management tasks. Running a TMO is akin to running a medium-sized business with an annual turnover in most cases of hundreds of thousands of pounds. So, as well as housing management, the development programme must focus on the general management skills of the tenants' organisation. These fall into two main parts:

First, the development programme needs to focus the committee's attention on staffing the TMO. There are three main possibilities. The first is for the committee to carry out the day-to-day management tasks itself and employ no staff. Alternatively staff may be directly employed, or a management agent may be contracted to undertake day-to-day management on the TMO's behalf. A combination of these options is also possible.

The prospect of employing staff directly means that the TMO will need training in recruitment and selection. Decisions must also be made about advertising for staff. The committee also needs training or its role as an employer. This should cover issues such as conditions of service, staff training, appraisal, discipline and dismissal, which are recognised as being particularly difficult for voluntary committees.

Second, there are a large number of general management skills that need to be attained. These include financial control and budgeting, performance monitoring, and an understanding of management systems. Additional areas requiring attention are the use of information technology and the management of contracts.

In addition to management skills, preparation to run a housing organisation should also include equal opportunities training.

### 7. Negotiating the Agreement

Concluding the management agreement with the local authority is likely to demand extensive negotiation to arrive at a position which suits both parties. In the development programme this demands two activities; training in negotiation and the actual negotiations themselves. Management and maintenance allowances, the availability of office premises, and the arrangements made concerning their financing and management will also require negotiation. Some additional training needs may also be identified during the negotiation period, and these should be met.

### 8. Assessing Competence

The agency retains its key role in assessing the prospect of a TMO emerging from the development programme. If, for whatever reason, at any stage the agency sees no likelihood of a fully-operational TMO emerging, the Department of the Environment requires that the development programme should be curtailed. This responsibility requires regular review of the TMO's progress and the committee's competence, which should be specifically reported in the development programme report.

### 9. The Development Programme Report

Before the proposal to establish a TMO is taken to a vote, the agency must prepare a report on the development of the TMO. At the latest, this must be produced within two years of the start of the development process. This report should include, as a minimum the items in Table 6.

*Table 6   The development report*

1. *Introduction*
   - previous promotion and feasibility work, and its outcomes

2. *The Development Programme*
   - objectives
   - work programme
   - training undertaken
   - tenants' views of training

3. *The Management Agreement*
   - Assessment of negotiation process
   - Summary of the proposed terms of the agreement

4. *The TMO's Competence*
   - individual competence
   - group competence
   - organisational competence

5. *Relationship with the Local Authority*

6. *Any Concerns or Unresolved Problems*

7. *Conclusions and Recommendations*

The full text of the management agreement and other relevant appendices should be included.

If the local authority is satisfied that the TMO is competent to manage, and that the management agreement is properly drafted, it must arrange for a ballot of tenants to be carried out within three months of receiving the development report.

### 10. Assessing Tenants' Support

Since the TMO is a resident-controlled organisation it is vital to maintain and encourage the continued support of tenants for the TMO proposals as they develop. This demands regular outreach work among uninvolved tenants, for example by means of public meetings, open days, exhibitions, and surveys.

Following a satisfactory development report which supports the setting up of a TMO, it is necessary to make arrangements for a ballot. The proposal to establish a

TMO must be notified to every tenant. The publicity must give a summary of the proposed management agreement, and a full copy of the agreement must be available for inspection on demand by tenants. The agency should then prepare the ballot paper which will ask whether or not tenants support the TMO. A good turnout is essential. The ballot must be secret and can be conducted door-to-door, by post or by using a polling station.

**11. Setting up the TMO**

If a majority of those eligible to vote approve the TMO, the management agreement must be formally signed with the council within three months of the ballot result. The final stage of the development programme is to carry out a range of practical tasks in order to get the TMO running. There is a great deal of work to be done in the handover period. This includes:

- finalising the TMO's management and committee structures
- setting up and equipping the office
- recruiting staff
- establishing systems of record-keeping and administration
- arranging for the handover of functions from the council. This may be a staged process
- publicising and launching the TMO

**12. Communication**

Communication remains a vital activity during the development programme. As with the feasibility stage there are two main targets; the tenants on the estate, and the local authority.

Tenants should be kept in touch with the developing TMO by regular meetings and newsletters. Communication with the local authority on progress should feature as an explicit part of the programme. In many cases, agencies and tenants' groups will want to involve the local authority in training, as well as keeping them in touch with developments.

**13. Monitoring**

As with the feasibility study, monitoring should be built into the development programme. As well as monitoring competence, it is essential for the tenants' group and the agency together to monitor the progress of the programme against its plan, and to adjust it if necessary to accommodate altered circumstances. The Department of the Environment requires regular progress reports and statements of estimated expenditure. End-of-year accounts for the development programme need to be externally audited by a qualified person.

Again, it is also essential that the committee monitors the agency's work. This is more important at this stage than during the feasibility study, because the responsibility of running the programme lies formally with the tenants, not with the agency. The local authority's advice will be useful, provided all parties agree.

**TIME INPUTS TO DEVELOPMENT PROGRAMMES**

Adequate time must be devoted to each of the key components of development programmes. While the tenants' committee's time is unpriced, the agency's time input must be specified in the bid for funding to carry out the work programmes and in any subsequent re-application. The time available to be spent on the programme by the agency depends on three factors: the size of the estate (which drives the Department of the Environment's formula for the maximum allowable expenditure); the time devoted to travelling as a proportion of the total input; and the hourly rate of the agency. These factors mean that there can be considerable variation between the time available for preparation and delivery of the programmes.

In spite of this variety, there is little point in providing a framework for the content of the work programme without also giving some guidance on the necessary time input for each of the essential components. Table 7 lays out suggested minimum and maximum proportions of time (including travel, preparation and meeting time) to be spent on each of the key components of development programmes. Normally, the time the agency devotes to each component in the development programme should fall between these limits. The principle is illustrated by a 600 hour development programme.

## PRESENTATION OF DEVELOPMENT PROGRAMMES

Appendix 3 provides an example of how a work programme should be laid out. This style of presentation is designed to make the components of the programme and their incidence over time explicit. It provides an easily-readable overview of the programme which can be used for planning and monitoring purposes by tenants, agencies, and the Department of the Environment.

The activities shown in the programme are not intended to be definitive—the detailed content of the programme will be planned according to the needs of the tenants and their estate.

Development programmes are longer than feasibility studies and are subject to greater uncertainty: at the start of the programme only the first few months of the programme need to be expressed in detail. Proposed input hours by the agency can be added to each column and row to aid assessment and monitoring of programmes.

*Table 7* Development programmes: suggested minimum and maximum time inputs
Example based on a programme of 600 hours for an estate of 300 dwellings

| Component | Minimum Hours | % of Time | Maximum Hours | % of Time | Average Hours | % of Time |
|---|---|---|---|---|---|---|
| 1. Planning the Development Programme | 12 | 2 | 18 | 3 | 16 | 3 |
| 2. Agreeing the Group's structure and responsibilities | 15 | 2 | 36 | 6 | 24 | 4 |
| 3. Incorporating the TMO | 10 | 2 | 14 | 2 | 12 | 2 |
| 4. Introducing the Modular Management Agreement | 24 | 4 | 48 | 8 | 36 | 6 |
| 5. Working up Management Options | 84 | 14 | 132 | 22 | 100 | 17 |
| 6. Preparing to Run a Housing Organisation | 72 | 12 | 120 | 20 | 96 | 16 |
| 7. Negotiating the Management Agreement | 72 | 12 | 120 | 20 | 96 | 16 |
| 8. Assessing Competence | 10 | 2 | 16 | 3 | 14 | 2 |
| 9. The Development Programme Report | 9 | 1 | 18 | 3 | 10 | 2 |
| 10. Assessing Tenants' Support | 48 | 8 | 90 | 15 | 70 | 12 |
| 11. Setting up the TMO | 72 | 12 | 120 | 20 | 96 | 16 |
| 12. Communication | 15 | 2 | 30 | 5 | 20 | 3 |
| 13. Monitoring and Review | 7 | 1 | 18 | 3 | 10 | 2 |
| Total | 450 | 75 | 780 | 130 | 600 | 100 |

Note: Percentages have been rounded where necessary

# Chapter 4   Competence to Manage

**INTRODUCTION**

Guidance by the Secretary of State, under Regulation 7 of the Housing (Right to Manage) Regulations 1994 states that tenants' organisations have the Right to Manage if they can show that they are competent to manage the functions they wish to take over.

The idea of assessing competence is not new. Although tenant management organisations have not officially had to demonstrate that they are capable of managing housing functions in the past, both agencies and local authorities made informal assessments. Some local authorities had already developed detailed checklists of areas that they wished to be satisfied about, while others took a more general view.

Tenants' groups were concerned that different landlords could take widely different views of competence under the Right to Manage and this might result in some groups being refused the right, even though they may be more competent than a group which had been allowed to take over housing management responsibilities elsewhere.

It is important that similar criteria are applied to different TMOs in different parts of the country. There is a need for a common understanding of what competence is and what TMOs should be competent to do. There is also a need for a common method of assessment which can be applied by prospective TMOs, agencies and local authorities. The TMO competences set out a baseline for minimum levels of competence and criteria for assessment.

The existence of written down standards also means that tenants who wish to take over management of their homes know, from the outset, what they are expected to know and to be able to do. The competences can, and should, be used to help identify training needs, to measure progress and to make sure that the TMO remains effective once it is up and running.

**WHAT IS COMPETENCE?**

An organisation is made up of its structure, its tasks, its systems and its people. A competent organisation is one in which competent people, working together, are able to carry out tasks effectively by operating the organisations' policies and systems. There are three elements to competence:

- individual competence
- group competence
- organisational competence.

**Individual Competence**

To describe someone as competent is to say that they have the ability to do a particular task or job in a capable manner. There is an underlying assumption that a competent person has the skills and knowledge necessary to do the job. However, it is important to recognise that the assessment of competence is about measuring the ability to 'do' something, not just the knowledge of how to do it.

**Group Competence**

While individuals in the organisation may have skills and abilities, these may not always be used. It is important that the TMO committee works together to manage the organisation. The TMO should be able to demonstrate this by the time the development report is submitted.

**Organisational Competence**

The competence of the organisation can be assessed by looking at its policies and systems and how these are carried out. These should comply with equal opportunities, legal requirements and recognised good practice.

**EXISTING MODELS**

Within the housing field, there are a variety of models for assessing the competence of individuals and housing organisations. The team drawing up the TMO competences looked at a wide variety of these to see if there were models which could be adapted for TMOs. The most useful models are outlined below.

**Key Task Analysis**

The *Training for Tenant Management* research identified the tasks which tenants developing a TMO need to do at each stage in the process and what the TMO committee needs to do once the organisation has taken over responsibility for management. The task analysis also identified the skills, knowledge and attitudes which tenants need to carry out these tasks effectively.

This analysis, which was tested in a variety of TMOs, formed the background for what TMOs need to do but more work was required to find ways of assessing competence.

**NVQs**

National Vocational Qualifications (NVQs) are a system of nationally recognised work-place based qualifications. They look at people's ability to do their jobs. NVQs cover a wide range of jobs including housing, general management, finance, building and training. They are based on units, which can be assessed at different levels and are, therefore, very flexible and adaptable. Although not designed for voluntary committees, they cover many of the skills and abilities needed by committee members.

Many TMO committee members interviewed in the *Training for Tenant Management* research expressed an interest in using what they had learnt to get a qualification, although they did not want to be forced to get a qualification. Some had already looked at NVQs as a way of getting recognition for the training and practical experience they had undertaken.

**Housing Association Performance Standards**

Housing associations are run by voluntary committees and many, particularly community based associations, develop in a similar way to TMOs. In order to get grants, associations must be registered with the Housing Corporation. The Corporation has a responsibility for ensuring that associations manage their affairs properly and adhere to good practice. Before an association can be registered, the Housing Corporation carries out a visit to ensure that the new association is ready to take over responsibility for managing houses. The Corporation also monitors established housing associations.

The Corporation's criteria for performance are published so that associations can monitor themselves. The performance expectations include:

- committee accountability
- management control
- financial control
- racial equality
- access to housing
- housing management services
- tenant participation.

These look both at the committee and at the policies, procedures and systems of the organisation. These standards are very relevant to TMOs.

**Local Authority Checklists**

A number of local authorities already assess whether TMOs in their area are ready to take over responsibility for housing management functions. Those examined tended to concentrate on ensuring that policies, procedures and systems were in place prior to handover.

**Using the Models**

The TMO competences have drawn on these four models to produce a set of baseline criteria. The competences recognise that tenant management organisations vary, both in size and in the functions they choose to take responsibility for. In some tenant management organisations, committee members carry out the day-to-day tasks involved in delivering housing services. In others, the TMO employs a team of staff and the committee's role here is to act as a board of directors.

The competences are, therefore, designed to be flexible, with 'core' and 'optional' elements, depending on which functions the TMO plans to take over and the level of involvement of the committee in the day-to-day running of the organisation. The next section looks at what the competences cover.

**WHAT DO TMOs NEED TO BE COMPETENT TO DO?**

The process of developing competence is continuous and ongoing. Few people have all the skills, knowledge and abilities they need when they first take on a new job and these must be learned as they go along through training and practical experience.

The individual competences have been designed to be built up in stages through the programmes of training and activities carried out in the feasibility study and development programme (described in Chapters 2 and 3). Organisational policies and systems will also be gradually put in place. The key areas of competence, at each stage are identified below and described in greater detail in Appendices 4, 5, 6 and 7.

**Feasibility**

At the feasibility stage, the programme (detailed in Chapter 2) covers a range of tasks. Tenants need the ability to:

- work together as a team
- assess their own training needs
- plan and review activities
- assess options

- contribute to the consultation process
- exercise financial control
- select an agency for the development stage.

In organisational terms, the tenants' organisation should be able to show that it is democratic, accountable, and representative through evidence that the constitution has been adhered to. The committee should be able to show that it is operating good practice and that systems for financial control are in place.

## Development

The major task at the development stage is for the TMO to decide which functions it wishes to manage and the levels of responsibility desired. Decisions on these issues will be taken as the tenants' committee makes choices from the Modular Management Agreement.

The TMO must be competent to manage each of the functions it chooses to take on and the range of competences required will, therefore, vary. The depth of competence needed will depend on how much tenants aim to do themselves. However, there are a range of tasks which all TMO committees must do, whether they are a policymaking body or deeply involved in the day-to-day business of delivering services. The competences at the development stage are, therefore, divided into 'core' competences and 'optional' competences.

### *Core Competences*

The core competences, which the TMO committee needs, are concerned with the management and control of the TMO. This includes being able to exercise financial control; plan, monitor and review activities; establish and maintain working relationships (both within and outside the organisation) and maintain communications with the residents of the area.

Some of these abilities will have been developed during the feasibility stage. Others will be developed during the development stage, as tenants take more control of the process. This includes taking responsibility for the budget; having greater involvement in the planning of training; and drawing up and negotiating the management agreement.

The key abilities are to:

- run effective meetings
- plan and evaluate training
- develop housing policies
- plan, control and negotiate budgets
- present information
- negotiate and monitor housing services
- establish and maintain working relationships with other organisations.

### *Optional Competences*

The optional competences required depend on which of three staffing options the TMO chooses to deliver the housing service. The options are:

- carry out the tasks themselves, or

- employ their own staff, or
- use a managing agency on contract.

Some TMOs have chosen to do all three. For example, a TMO may employ a housing manager to administer many of the day-to-day services, use the services of an accountant, through a contract, to administer the finances and also carry out some tasks themselves. If the TMO intends to employ staff and/or use contractors to deliver services, committee members must have the ability to select and manage staff and manage service contracts.

The choice of how much involvement the committee has in day-to-day activities must be made by the tenants themselves. As a voluntary and unpaid committee they are often giving up considerable time to be involved in the TMO. However, both the tenants and the local authority will want to be sure that the TMO committee has the ability to carry out the level and range of functions effectively.

Where tenants themselves are delivering the day-to-day services such as interviewing applicants, taking repair requests, ordering repair work and giving advice, they are acting as housing officers. They need to have the knowledge and abilities of competent housing officers to carry out these tasks effectively. The optional competences for day-to-day management are:

- ability to control budgets and finance
- ability to provide information for clients
- ability to communicate housing policies, programmes and services
- ability to let properties
- ability to organise repairs and maintenance
- ability to plan, organise and evaluate work.

The optional competences can be considered as a menu. Tenants should become competent in the functions which they will be doing. They do not need to acquire competences in areas which will be completely delegated to staff or agents. However, they may need to meet part of the criteria if they have some level of involvement. For example, in many TMOs, a sub-committee of tenants carries out interviews of applicants for housing but the housing manager administers the waiting list and the letting procedure. The committee members involved in this should be able to demonstrate that they are interviewing people in accordance with TMO policy and taking account of legal and equal opportunities issues.

*Organisational Competence*

By the time the agency submits its development report, the TMO should have chosen, negotiated and agreed its management options with the local authority. Policies and procedures which form appendices to the agreement should also have been drawn up.

Although there will still be much work to do to set up the organisation, the policies and procedures in the management agreement form the basis for assessing organisational competence.

Although the functions taken on will vary, all TMOs should be able to demonstrate that committee structures are in place and that policies and procedures for financial control and tenant involvement are in operation.

## WHO SHOULD BE COMPETENT?

Within any group, different people will play different roles. Individual abilities, motivation and commitment vary widely. There are some competences which all committee members need (such as the ability to work as a team member) but there are others which only some committee members need.

The approach we have taken recognises that different levels of competence may exist but that the group, as a whole, may be considered competent provided that all the skills and knowledge required are present.

Although most TMOs have a Chairperson, Secretary and Treasurer, the roles of individual office bearers vary widely. The competences are not, therefore, linked to individual posts. However, it is important that, for example, the person handling finance is competent (whether or not that person is the designated treasurer).

Because the important thing is that the group, as a whole, should between them have the necessary skills and abilities, competences may be shared by several individuals. The ability to run effective meetings, for example, may be shared between the Chairperson and Secretary who would both have roles to play.

### *Dealing with Turnover of Committee Members*

In some committees, the membership of the group remains fairly stable over a long period of time; in others there is a high turnover in active members. In any organisation, people may leave and new members may join. In a TMO, committee members may stand down or leave the area.

The competences have been designed to be robust enough so that if some committee members leave, key abilities, necessary to effective management, are not lost. While, as a minimum, only one person may be required to have a particular competence, it is preferable that several people develop critical abilities. This will ensure that if key people leave, others are in a position to take over the responsibilities with a minimum of disruption. *Learning to Manage* suggests that TMOs create assistant posts, such as Vice-Chair, Minutes Secretary and Assistant Treasurer. People in these positions would share some of the duties and stand in as necessary. Creation of such posts also helps to spread the workload of the committee more evenly.

It is also recommended that the TMO ensures that it is not over-reliant on one or two key people who hold all the competences.

In some TMOs, there have been occasions when almost the entire committee membership has been voted out at the annual elections. The incoming committee members may have many existing and relevant abilities. But, in such circumstances, the competence of the organisation overall would need to be reassessed.

There are some ways of overcoming the problems that this possibility may cause. First, during development, such severe lack of confidence by the membership should be foreseeable. Efforts should be made to involve the wider membership in activities and training to ensure a pool of competent individuals.

Second, while the democratic process of elections must take place, efforts should be made to plan for the AGM to take place well in advance of the handover period so that new members can learn the skills and knowledge required.

## WHO SHOULD ASSESS COMPETENCE?

Guidance by the Secretary of State under Regulation 7 of the Housing (Right to Manage) Regulations 1994 indicates that the responsibility for assessing the competence of the TMO lies with the approved agency working with the group.

Ideally, the tenants, the agency and the local authority should work in partnership to develop the TMO. In this way, local authority officers would be closely involved in training and would be able to form their assessment of the TMO's competence. Legally, the local authority has the right to challenge the agency's view that the TMO is competent and an arbitration procedure is built into the Regulations.

It is important that the agency has the ability to assess competence. In order to ensure this, the Department of the Environment has a list of approved agencies who can demonstrate their competence to take on work involved in setting up a TMO. The approval procedure for agencies is set out in *The Guide to the Right to Manage*.

Agencies may particularly wish to note that there is a National Vocational Qualification (NVQ) unit of competence as an assessor (Housing NVQ Level 4, Unit B3 — Assess Candidate Using Diverse Evidence). Agency staff may find this useful.

# Chapter 5  Assessing Competence

**INTRODUCTION**

The assessment of competence of a TMO is a three part process. The agent should assess

- individual competence
- group competence
- that organisational policies and procedures are in place.

This chapter sets out how competence should be assessed.

**INDIVIDUAL COMPETENCE**
**When Assessment Should Take Place**

The assessment of individual competence should be a continuous activity, linked to training and the work programme. The guide to training for tenant management, *Learning to Manage*, suggests that tenants and their agencies should use the TMO competences as a tool to assess training needs at the beginning of each stage. This would be done by assessing what individuals can do at the outset.

The gap between what individuals already know and can do and what they need to know and do identifies the areas which should form the basis of the training programme (the TMO's 'training needs').

It is quite possible that some committee members may already be competent in particular areas, as a result of their previous work, family and voluntary experiences. If this is the case, and the competence area is one which is only needed by a small number of committee members, then less emphasis would be placed on this in training.

Training needs must be kept under regular review, particularly if new people join the group, office bearers change or the situation changes.

The agency's assessment of the TMO will not be a test or exam: the assessment will take place as a natural part of training and development programme activities.

**The Layout of the Competences**

The competences for individuals are broken down into areas of activity at the feasibility and development stages (see Appendices 4, 5 and 6). For each area of competence there is a standard set of components, as shown in Table 8.

**HOW INDIVIDUAL COMPETENCE SHOULD BE ASSESSED**

The assessment of competence can be carried out in a number of different ways. These include:

- observation
- description
- individual meetings

- different circumstances
- written information
- evidence from other people.

*Table 8* Layout of the competences

| | |
|---|---|
| Title: | The description of the activity, given as an ability to do the set of tasks |
| Why Needed?: | The reason why the area of competence has been included |
| What Does it Include?: | Some complex tasks have a number of elements. These are identified |
| Who Needs the Ability?: | This heading indicates whether all the committee, some of the committee or only one person needs to have the competence |
| Example: | An example of the activity in practice |
| What Will be Assessed?: | This section describes what the individual should be able to do in more detail. This section and the following component on knowledge are the key parts of the competence as they define the performance required |
| What Supporting Knowledge is Needed: | To carry out tasks effectively, people need an underlying knowledge of legislation, and the policies and procedures of the organisation. This section details these for each competence |
| NVQ Alternative: | The TMO competences are adapted from the Housing National Vocational Qualifications (NVQs). This section notes the NVQ units which most closely match the TMO competence |

**Observation**

Direct observation is the best method of assessing competence. As the agency working with a tenants' committee, there will be many opportunities to see individuals in action — putting their skills and knowledge into practice. The types of activities which may be observed and assessed include:

- exercises and role-play during training
- committee meetings
- negotiations with the local authority
- sessions developing the management agreement.

This type of assessment can be quite informal.

**Description**

Although direct observation is preferred, the agency will not see all the activities carried out. Some evidence of competence can be obtained from review meetings in which particular activities are evaluated by the group.

**Individual Meetings**

For some competences, particularly those which are specialised, the agency may need to have a meeting with committee members on an individual basis. These need not necessarily be separate from other activities. It is likely that, during the course of work programmes, the agent will meet with individual tenants, particularly office bearers, to discuss and plan business or to give one to one coaching sessions.

**Different Circumstances**

During both group and individual sessions (including training sessions) a useful assessment method is to ask what people would do in different circumstances. This can be done through role-play or presenting different scenarios ('What would you do if....?') This method can indicate both whether skills and knowledge can be transferred to other situations or find whether people would know how to deal with problems they have not encountered (but might in the future).

**Written Information**

During the course of the feasibility and development programmes, the TMO is likely to have produced a wealth of paperwork. This may include committee minutes, newsletters, letters, policies and financial statements. This evidence can be used to support other evidence of competence.

**Evidence from Other People**

There are likely to be a number of people who have seen members of the TMO in action and are able to give their views of competence. These include local authority officers, other trainers, other committee members and directly employed staff. Such evidence should be used sensitively and never as the only source, but these views can provide a valuable additional source of feedback.

**GROUP COMPETENCE**

Having looked at the abilities of individual committee members and assessed their competence over the range of activities, the next step is to look at the group as a whole. The TMO committee has a *collective* responsibility for all the activities and functions of the organisation. The committee, as a group, must have the capacity, commitment and experience to manage the organisation effectively.

The following questions should be addressed.

1. **Does the TMO committee, as a whole, have the range of abilities and knowledge required to manage the organisation?**
This question should be answered by reference to the individual competences. Between them, the committee members' abilities and knowledge should cover the functions for which the TMO will be responsible and its overall management responsibilities. Ideally, there should be a spread of skills and knowledge, rather than a concentration in a small group.

2. **Is effective control exercised by the committee as a whole?**
It is important that the committee works together as a group. Decisions should involve the committee, as a whole, and should not be made by one individual or a small group within the committee. Effective control also includes ensuring that meetings are properly conducted, and that activities are planned and reviewed.

3. **Are TMO committee members committed to the objectives of the organisation and do they have sufficient time and energy to devote to the work involved?**
Control cannot be exercised by people who are never there, or only appear occasionally. In addition, committee members, particularly the office bearers, should do more than simply turn up to meetings. The amount of time required will depend on how much work the committee intends to carry out itself rather than delegate to officers or agents.

4. **Does the structure of the organisation enable the TMO committee to control its activities, implement its responsibilities and meet its objectives?**
The TMO should have set up appropriate sub-committees and working parties with clear responsibilities and reporting systems. These should comply with the TMO's rules (or Articles of Association).

5. **Does the TMO committee ensure that all policies, procedures and practices comply with equal opportunities obligations, relevant legal requirements and recognised good practice?**

Although these are stressed in individual competences, it is important that the committee, as a whole, is committed to ensuring that its collective actions have regard to these issues.

6. **Does the composition of the TMO committee reflect the composition of the area?**

The committee must be seen to representative of the community which it serves. There should be a balance of gender, race, age and religion as far as possible. If this does not occur naturally, then the committee should take steps to encourage and co-opt additional members.

**ORGANISATIONAL CHECKLISTS**

Chapter 4 indicated that an organisation is made up of people and systems. These systems include the policies and procedures which have been agreed by the organisation. If followed, the policies and procedures ensure that the organisation will operate effectively.

Ensuring that suitable systems are in place is, therefore, no less important than ensuring that the committee has the skills and abilities to manage the organisation. Like individual competences, the policies and procedures will be built up gradually.

In order to serve a notice seeking the Right to Manage, the tenants' organisation must have some basic policies and procedures in place. These would be largely contained in the constitution and standing orders of the organisation.

By the end of the feasibility stage, there should be evidence to show that the TMO has been operating in accordance with its constitution.

During the development stage, many more policies and procedures will be established as decisions are made about the management agreement and its contents.

The TMO competences contain a checklist of minimum organisational requirements which are needed for each stage. At the development stage, the checklist is divided into 'core' policies and procedures for areas such as committee operation, tenant participation and financial control and 'options' — which will depend on the functions being taken on.

After the development report, there is a further element of work to establish the TMO (see Chapter 3). This includes setting up and equipping the office and establishing systems for record-keeping and administration. Before the TMO takes over responsibility for managing the functions agreed, it should ensure that everything is in place. A final checklist of policies, procedures and systems is included in *The Guide to the Right to Manage*. This is not part of the assessment of competence but is intended as guidance to TMOs and local authorities.

**REPORTING ON COMPETENCE**
**Feasibility Stage**

Under the Right to Manage Regulations, the agency has a specific duty to report on the TMO's progress in the feasibility report. If, in the agency's opinion, the TMO is unlikely to progress towards full tenant management, the agency should submit an early feasibility report setting out the reasons for bringing the study to an early conclusion. Such reasons could include that the TMO:

- is not operating in accordance with its constitution
- is pursuing tenant management in order to exclude certain sections of the community
- has a committee or board which is not reasonably representative of all sections of the community, and has to plans no remedy this.

The individual, group and organisational competences are clearly relevant here. The early report should make specific reference to the areas where performance is unsatisfactory.

Assuming that an early report is not required, the feasibility report should include a section about the TMO and its committee (see Table 3). This section should confirm that:

a) individual competences have been achieved by the required number of people

b) the group, as a whole, meet the group competence criteria

c) the TMO can fulfil the items on the organisational checklist.

If any of these cannot be demonstrated, the agency should comment on steps needed. This could include further training, recruiting more committee members or improving policies and procedures.

## Development Stage

At the development stage, the agency must confirm, in the development report, that the TMO is competent to carry out its responsibilities under the proposed management agreement. Again, an early report should be submitted if the TMO's performance raises doubts that the organisation could assume the range of management functions it wishes to take on.

The section of the development report on the competence of the TMO (see Table 6) should detail the individual, group and organisational competences achieved.

# Appendix 1   Summary of Research Methods

**1. TMO COMPETENCES
Research Aims and Objectives**

The aim of the TMO competences project was to produce a nationally recognised set of baseline competences which could be understood and applied by prospective TMOs, agencies and local authorities.

The objectives were to provide:

i) a recognised set of skills and abilities required for running a tenant management organisation and, in particular, the housing it controls

ii) measures for all the skills and abilities required by organisations and key individuals for taking over management of their housing, including

iii) measures that reflect the fact that there will be several levels of competence and that they are flexible enough to be applicable to tenant management organisations at different stages of development

iv) measures that can be applied by local authorities, training agencies and prospective TMOs, and

v) an inventory of the skills and abilities which are required for a prospective TMO to proceed through each stage of promotion and development towards ongoing management.

**Methods**

The skills and abilities which members of a TMO need to successfully manage their homes have been derived from research carried out by the University of Glasgow and TPAS (Scotland). The research report *Training for Tenant Management* includes lists of key tasks, knowledge, skills and abilities required by TMOs at different stages of promotion and development.

The competences project built on these lists and tested them further to ensure that they were robust in a wide variety of settings. The work included:

i) interviews with 35 local authority officers, members of TMOs, agency workers and specialists in competence work

ii) observation of the activities of seven TMOs at various stages of feasibility and development

iii) submitting drafts to an Advisory Group of representatives from agencies, TMOs, the local authority associations, the Chartered Institute of Housing, the Local Government Management Board, local authorities and Universities for comment

iv) receiving feedback from several seminars and workshops, where participants included local authority staff, Section 16 funded agencies and tenants involved in established and prospective TMOs

v) testing the draft competences by carrying out pilot assessments in five TMOs at various stages of feasibility and development.

## 2. FRAMEWORKS FOR FEASIBILITY STUDIES AND DEVELOPMENT PROGRAMMES

**Aims and Objectives**

The aim of the frameworks project was to produce 'model feasibility and development programmes' for use by agencies and tenants' groups seeking to progress towards a TMO.

The objectives were:

i) to produce programmes which contain a 'core' of essential tasks, skills, and knowledge at each stage, which would apply to all TMOs irrespective of the number or range of delegated management responsibilities they take over from the local authority

ii) to produce programmes which are clearly embedded in the work undertaken on the Modular Management Agreement, TMO competences and training quality assessment.

**Methods**

The frameworks for feasibility studies and development programmes were developed as follows.

i) Files relating to 20 training agencies and 20 development programmes were extracted from the Department of the Environment's records for analysis. These included both large and small agencies and programmes intended to lead to a variety of types of TMO. Files all related to 1992 and 1993.

ii) On the basis of these files, and the recommendations of the studies on *Training for Tenant Management* and TMO competences, draft model programmes were compiled.

iii) These model programmes were then validated to ensure their acceptance. Validation took place by three methods:

　　a) postal consultation in January 1994, with all approved agencies and all local authorities with current TMO development programmes

　　b) face-to-face interviews with a selection of training agencies and local authorities

　　c) discussion at an advisory group for the project comprised of representatives of TMOs, agencies and local authorities.

In addition, a draft of the components of the model programmes was discussed at two workshops for tenants, local authorities and agencies at the conference launching *Training for Tenant Management*.

iv) On the basis of the validation exercise, the programmes were finalised.

# Appendix 2  Example Programme: Feasibility Study

| Component | Month 1 | Month 2 | Month 3 |
|---|---|---|---|
| 1. Planning the Feasibility Study | Training: Feasibility Studies<br>Training: Planning training needs<br>Planning: Agreeing feasibility study | | |
| 2. Assessing the Estate's Problems and Priorities | | Collation of available data<br>Tenants forum/discussion groups | Assessment of physical problems<br>Meetings with council staff responsible for the estate |
| 3. Assessing the Support for Tenant Involvement | | Exhibition day, drop-in workshops | Survey of residents<br>Street or block meetings |
| 4. Exploring Management Options | Training: What kind of resident participation<br>Training: TMO options | Visit to TMO<br>Training: Transferred ownership option | Training: More intensive participation within existing structures |
| 5. Understanding Housing Management and Finance | | | Training: How the council works<br>Training: Introduction to Housing management |
| 6. Preparing for a Management Role | Training: Working as a tenants' committee | Training: Involving residents and equal opportunities | |
| 7. Assessing Competence | Training: Competences | | Interim assessment of competence |
| 8. The Feasibility Report | | | |
| 9. The 'Test of Opinion' | | | |
| 10. Planning for the Development Stage | | | |
| 11. Communication | Meeting with local authority<br>Public meeting: launch<br>Newsletter No. 1 | Liaison with local authority | Liaison with local authority<br>Newsletter No. 2. The exhibition day |
| 12. Monitoring | Agreement of monitoring criteria | | Monitoring meeting, agency and steering group -<br>Progress of programme, training needs |

| Month 4 | Month 5 | Month 6 |
|---|---|---|
| Additional surveys  Review of estate problems and priorities | | |
| Exhibition day in preparation for ballot | Ballot residents | |
| Agreement on preferred option | Training: Focused on preferred option | |
| Training: Housing finance | Training: Financing and managing a TMO | |
| Training: Negotiating skills | Training: Representing the community | |
| | Monitoring: Competences of group: future training needs | |
| Draft feasibility report and circulate | Finalise Feasibility Report | |
| | Ballot or poll for all tenants | |
| | | Training: Development programmes  Training: Selecting an agency  Training: Future training needs |
| Liaison with LA - preferred option  Public meeting - tenant management options and preferred option | Liaison with local authority  Newsletter No. 3 | Liaison with local authority: the development phase |
| | | Review of programme and success of agency |

# Appendix 3 Example Programme: Development Programme

| Component | Month 1 | Month 2 | Month 3 |
|---|---|---|---|
| 1. Planning the Development Programme | Training: Development programme<br>Training: Planning training needs<br>Planning: Agreeing development programme | | |
| 2. Agreeing the Group's Structure & Responsibilities | Training: Management structures<br>Agreement on structure and responsibilities | Training: Office bearer's roles | |
| 3. Incorporating the TMO | | Training: Constitution of TMOs | Registration of TMO |
| 4. Introducing the Modular Management Agreement | | Training: The management agreement | Training: Management functions and level of responsibility |
| 5. Working up Management Options | | | Training: Repairs |
| 6. Preparing to run a Housing Organisation | | Training: Equal opportunities | Training: Financial management |
| 7. Negotiating the Management Agreement | | | |
| 8. Assessing Competence | Training: Competences | | |
| 9. The Development Programme Report | | | |
| 10. Assessing Tenants' Support | | Membership recruitment drive | Membership drive continued |
| 11. Setting up the TMO | | | |
| 12. Communication | Newsletter<br>Meeting with local authority | | Public meeting<br>Meeting with local authority |
| 13. Monitoring | Establish monitoring criteria and meetings | Assessment of structures and office bearers | Quarterly review of programme |

| Month 4 | Month 5 | Month 6 |
|---|---|---|
| Training: Rents | Training: Tenancy management | Training: Allocations |
| Training: Performance Review | Training: IT | |
| Catch-up training for new members | Catch-up training for new members | Training: Staffing |
| | | Interim review of competences |
| | Discussion groups - tenant priorities | |
| Newsletter | Meeting with LA | |
| | Review of programme for months 7-12 | Quarterly review of programme |

| Component | Months 7-9 | Months 10-12 | Months 13-16 |
|---|---|---|---|
| 1. Planning the Development Programme | | | |
| 2. Agreeing the Group's Structure & Responsibilities | | | |
| 3. Incorporating the TMO | | | |
| 4. Introducing the Modular Management Agreement | | | |
| 5. Working up Management Options | Training: Other functions | Decision on preferred options | |
| 6. Preparing to run a Housing Organisation | Training: Contracts | | Additional training |
| 7. Negotiating the Management Agreement | Training: Negotiating the agreement | Negotiations | Negotiations |
| 8. Assessing Competence | | Interim review of competences | |
| 9. The Development Programme Report | | | |
| 10. Assessing Tenants' Support | | Exhibition day<br>Public meetings | |
| 11. Setting up the TMO | | Establishment of office | |
| 12. Communication | Newsletters<br>TMO: the proposals<br>Meeting with LA:<br>Proposals for TMO | | Newsletters |
| 13. Monitoring | Quarterly review of programme | Review of progress to competence<br>Quarterly review of programme | Annual audit of accounts<br>Quarterly review of programme |

| Months 17-20 | Months 21-24 |

Additional training

　　　　　　　　　　　　　　Training: Management for real

Conclusion of Negotiations　　Signing the agreement

Final assessment of TMO
competences

Drafting and finalising the report

Ballot of tenants　　　　　　Membership drive

Staff recruitment　　　　　　Setting up the office
　　　　　　　　　　　　　　Setting up administrative systems

Newsletters　　　　　　　　Newsletters
　　　　　　　　　　　　　　Public launch of TMO

Assessment of TMO competence　　Audit of accounts
Quarterly review of programme

# Appendix 4  TMO Competences

F1  Ability to work as a team member

F2  Ability to assess own training needs

F3  Ability to plan and review activities

F4  Ability to assess options

F5  Ability to contribute to consultation process

F6  Ability to exercise financial control

F7  Ability to select an agency for the development stage

F8  Organisational Checklist

**Feasibility 1: Ability to Work as a Team Member**

Why Needed?: This ability underpins everything else
The tenants' committee must be able to show that it is an effective group

Who Needs the Ability?: All committee members

What Does it Include?: Develop and maintain constructive working relationships with colleagues

Example: The committee shows that sexist or racist remarks are not acceptable behaviour

What Will be Assessed?: The agency will assess whether committee members:
a) take time to develop constructive working relationships with each other
b) provide information in an appropriate manner
c) deal with differences of opinion in ways which avoid offence
d) deal with breakdowns in relationships in an appropriate way
e) set clear standards of behaviour within the group and follow these

What Supporting Knowledge is Needed?: Effective team work
Committee members' roles and responsibilities
Equal opportunities
Communication skills

NVQ Alternative: Housing NVQ level 2 Unit 6.1

| | | |
|---|---|---|
| **Feasibility 2: Ability to Assess Own Training Needs** | Why Needed?: | Training programmes should be based on an assessment of what individuals need to learn |
| | Who Needs the Ability?: | All committee members |
| | What Does it Include?: | 1) Identify skills and knowledge required<br>2) Identify own strengths and weaknesses |
| | Example: | Committee members discuss training needs with agency worker in individual interviews |
| | What Will be Assessed?: | The agency will assess whether committee members:<br>a) can compare current abilities with competences needed<br>b) identify areas of training required<br>c) review own progress and performance<br>d) use feedback to improve performance<br>e) accept responsibility for achieving own training objectives |
| | What Supporting Knowledge is Needed?: | TMO competences<br>Personal strengths and weaknesses<br>TMO policies and plans<br>Feasibility and development programmes |
| | NVQ Alternative: | Housing NVQ Level 3 Unit B2.4 |

| **Feasibility 3: Ability to Plan and Review Activities** | Why Needed?: By the end of the feasibility programme, the tenants' committee must be able to show that it can plan work and monitor progress |
|---|---|

Who Needs the Ability?: All committee members should contribute

What Does it Include?:
1) Agree work objectives
2) Plan activities
3) Contribute to decision making
4) Review progress

Example: The tenants' committee works with the agency to plan the feasibility study and monitor progress

What Will be Assessed?: The agency will assess whether committee members:
a) agree objectives which are in line with the organisation's aims
b) plan activities in consultation with others
c) present suggestions clearly and in an appropriate way
d) review progress and use what has been learnt to plan future activities
e) take appropriate action if objectives have not been achieved

What Supporting Knowledge is Needed?:
Right to Manage Regulations and Circular
What a feasibility study is
Aims of tenants' organisation
Committee members' role
Assertiveness skills
Equal opportunities issues

NVQ Alternative: Housing NVQ Level 2 Unit 2

| **Feasibility 4: Ability to Assess Options** | | |
|---|---|---|

| | | |
|---|---|---|
| Why Needed?: | | This competence assesses the ability to obtain information, weigh up different alternatives and reach a decision. The TMO must show that it can make effective decisions based on sufficient information |
| Who Needs the Ability?: | | All committee members should contribute |
| What Does it Include?: | | 1) Obtain information<br>2) Assess information<br>3) Decide on a course of action |
| Example: | | The tenants' committee learns about alternative options, discusses the pros and cons and decides on a particular option which meets the needs of their area |
| What Will be Assessed?: | | The agency will assess whether committee members:<br>a) identify sources of information and assess them for usefulness, reliability and cost<br>b) take opportunities to establish contact with people who can provide information<br>c) seek alternative sources if there is not enough information available<br>d) discuss the pros and cons of alternative options and relate these to problems and priorities in the area<br>e) agree on a course of action, in accordance with legal requirement and TMO policy |
| What Supporting Knowledge is Needed?: | | Aims of tenants' organisation<br>Awareness of options available<br>Estate problems and priorities<br>Understanding of housing management and finance<br>Equal opportunities issues |
| NVQ Alternative: | | Housing NVQ Level 2 Unit 4/Level 2 Unit 1 |

**Feasibility 5: Ability to Contribute to Consultation Process**

Why Needed?: The TMO must show that it can consult residents. This competence shows that committee members can ensure that the consultation process meets the needs of the area. The actual organisation and carrying out of consultation may be done by others

Who Needs the Ability?: Several committee members should have this ability

What Does it Include?:
1) Identify people who need to be consulted
2) Identify appropriate methods of consultation
3) Ensure that consultation is organised effectively
4) Evaluate and review events

Example: A sub-committee works with the agency to organise public meetings, exhibitions and newsletters

What Will be Assessed?: The agency will assess whether committee members:
a) identify all the people who should be consulted
b) assess the pros and cons of different methods
c) suggest methods which are appropriate for the area and within budget
d) identify possible barriers to communication and suggest solutions
e) ensure that written information is accurate
f) ensure that venues for meetings are suitable for the people attending
g) monitor and review the consultation in process
h) where improvements are identified, make suggestions to the appropriate people

What Supporting Knowledge is Needed?: Awareness of tenant participation issues
Awareness of equal opportunities issues
Procedures and good practice in organising meetings
Preparation and presentation of newsletters
Feasibility work programme

NVQ Alternative: Housing NVQ Level 2 Unit 3

**Feasibility 6: Ability to Exercise Financial Control**

Why Needed?:
Although the TMO does not have financial responsibility for the Section 16 budget at the feasibility stage, it needs to demonstrate a minimum level of financial competence prior to moving on to the development stage. If the tenants' organisation has no money, financial systems should be set up and practised in training sessions

Who Needs the Ability?:
At least one committee member

What Does it Include?:
1) Keep financial records
2) Submit financial accounts

Example:
Treasurer manages tenants' organisation accounts, membership fees are collected and recorded

What Will be Assessed?:
The agency will assess whether the committee members:
a) update income records accurately
b) submit accurate financial reports
c) authorise payments in line with financial standing orders
d) maintain efficient financial systems

What Supporting Knowledge is Needed?:
Simple book-keeping systems
Good practice on financial issues
Role and responsibility of treasurer
Financial standing orders and constitution of organisation

NVQ Alternative:
Housing NVQ Level 3 Unit 7

**Feasibility 7: Ability to Select an Agency for the Development Stage**

| | |
|---|---|
| Why Needed?: | The TMO must select an agency for the development stage |
| | The selection procedure provides useful experience for the recruitment of staff and selection of contractors |
| Who Needs the Ability?: | Several members of the committee |
| What Does it Include?: | 1) Identify requirements |
| | 2) Draw up selection procedure |
| | 3) Interview candidates |
| | 4) Decide course of action |
| Example: | A sub-committee is set up to select, interview and appoint an agent for the development stage. The assessment of the interview and decision may be based on role-play |
| What Will be Assessed?: | a) draw up a brief which takes work objectives and known constraints into account |
| | b) identify the skills, knowledge and abilities that they are looking for |
| | c) draw up a selection procedure which conforms with suggested good practice |
| | d) take equal opportunities and other legal requirements into account |
| | e) ask questions which are relevant to the selection criteria |
| | f) base appointment decision on comparisons between information obtained and selection criteria |
| | g) assess value for money |
| What Supporting Knowledge is Needed?: | Awareness of Section 16 funding |
| | Role of agency as 'approved' person |
| | Key features of employment legislation |
| | Equal opportunities legislation |
| | Good practice in selection and recruitment |
| | TMO's policies, procedures and plans |
| | Understanding of training needs for the development stage |
| NVQ Alternative: | Housing NVQ Level 3 Unit B1 |

| **Feasibility 8:** |
| **Organisational Checklist** |

In order to serve a notice seeking the Right to Manage, the tenants' organisation must have a constitution which meets the conditions laid down by the Secretary of State, have a defined area and have at least 20 per cent of secure tenants in the area as members. The checklist seeks to ensure that the tenants' organisation is operating in accordance with its constitution; it also ensures that good practice in committee work and financial control are being observed.

### A. CONSTITUTION

1) Has a constitution which meets the conditions laid down by the Secretary of State been adopted? ☐
2) Is an accurate list of properties covered by the organisation available? ☐
3) Have office bearers (Chairperson, Secretary and Treasurer) been appointed? ☐
4) Are adequate standing orders available? ☐
5) Is an up-to-date record of membership kept? ☐
6) Has an annual report been produced and made available? ☐
7) Does the committee have an appropriate equal opportunities policy? ☐
8) Is there evidence that the equal opportunities policy is being implemented? ☐

### B. COMMITTEE

1) Are agendas produced and circulated in advance of committee meetings? ☐
2) Is incoming correspondence dealt with in accordance with standing orders? ☐
3) Is outgoing correspondence of appropriate quality produced with committee authority? ☐
4) Are adequate minutes produced from committee and general meetings? ☐
5) Are minutes circulated to the committee and filed adequately? ☐

### C. FINANCE

1) Are there appropriate finance policies and procedures? ☐
2) Have appropriate independent auditors been interviewed and appointed? ☐
3) Are up-to-date and accurate records kept of income and expenditure? ☐
4) Have cheque signatories been appointed in line with the constitution? ☐
5) Has a bank/building society account been set up? ☐
6) Is there a system for dealing with petty cash? ☐
7) (If appropriate) Are satisfactory audited accounts available? ☐

# Appendix 5   Core Development Competences

D1   Ability to run effective meetings

D2   Ability to plan and evaluate training

D3   Ability to develop housing policies

D4   Ability to plan, control and negotiate budgets

D5   Ability to present information—written and spoken

D6   Ability to establish and maintain working relationships with other organisations

D7   Ability to negotiate and monitor housing services

| **Development 1: Ability to Run Effective Meetings** | | |
|---|---|---|
| | Why Needed?: | The tenants' committee must be able to show that it can run business meetings in an organised way and ensure that everyone has opportunities to contribute |
| | Who Needs the Ability?: | At least one member of the committee, and preferably several, should have the ability to run meetings. Responsibilities may be split between committee members |
| | What Does it Include?: | 1) Organisation of suitable venues<br>2) Production of agendas and minutes<br>3) Effective chairing<br>4) Contributions to decision making |
| | Example: | Chairperson and Secretary organise a business meeting |
| | What Will be Assessed?: | The agency will assess whether committee members<br>a) ensure that the venue and seating arrangements are suitable for the type of meeting<br>b) ensure that agendas are sent out in advance<br>c) establish the purpose of the meeting clearly at the start<br>d) present information clearly and concisely<br>e) encourage all group members to make contributions<br>f) discourage wandering off the point and unhelpful arguments<br>g) ensure that decisions are within the groups' authority<br>h) ensure that accurate and clear minutes are taken |
| | What Supporting Knowledge is Needed?: | Tenants' organisation constitution and standing orders<br>Role of chairperson and secretary<br>Identify chairing skills<br>Identify secretarial skills<br>Conditions necessary for effective meetings |
| | NVQ Alternative: | Housing NVQ Level 4 Unit 2.4 |

| **Development 2: Ability to Plan and Evaluate Training** | | |
|---|---|---|
| | Why Needed?: | During the development stage, the committee should be more involved in planning training and evaluating whether it is effective |
| | Who Needs the Ability?: | All committee members should contribute |
| | What Does it Include?: | 1) Identify training needs of group<br>2) Assess suitability of training methods<br>3) Develop a training programme<br>4) Review and evaluate training received |
| | Example: | Committee members draw up training programme, in consultation with agency, to meet needs identified. Committee members complete questionnaire after training sessions |
| | What Will be Assessed?: | The agency will assess whether committee members:<br>a) identify the groups' overall training needs<br>b) contribute to discussions to plan how these needs will be met<br>c) take the TMO's objectives and work programme into account<br>d) assess the pros and cons of different training methods and relate these to individuals' preferred ways of learning<br>e) ensure value for money and cost-effective use of resources when planning training<br>f) monitor and review the training received regularly<br>g) make suggestions for areas where training could be improved |
| | What Supporting Knowledge is Needed?: | TMO's aims and objectives<br>Development work programme<br>TMO competences<br>Section 16 funding criteria<br>The range of training methods available<br>Equal opportunities issues and implications<br>Outline of Modular Management Agreement |
| | NVQ Alternative: | Housing NVQ Level 3 Unit B2 |

**Development 3: Ability to Develop Housing Policies**

Why Needed?: A major part of the development process concerns decisions about the functions which the TMO wishes to manage and the development of policies and procedures for these functions. These form part of the management agreement The TMO committee members must understand the underlying reasons for particular policies and procedures
Note that this competence is needed for each function the TMO plans to take on

Who Needs the Ability?: All committee members should develop the supporting knowledge
At least one committee member should have the ability to develop policies and procedures for each function (with professional assistance)

What Does it Include?:
1) Identify housing policy issues
2) Assess relevant information
3) Discuss housing policy options
4) Decide housing policies

Example: The TMO members may be part of a sub-committee or working group involved in drawing up policies for a particular function. This could involve:
—identifying key issues
—obtaining information from the local authority and other TMOs
—assessing examples of policies
—developing own policies

What Will be Assessed?: The agency will assess whether committee members:
a) identify issues which are relevant to the TMO
b) are able to support key issues by argument and evidence
c) take opportunities to contact people who can provide relevant information
d) discuss the pros and cons of different options and relate these to problems and priorities in the area
e) take account of local authority policies and views
f) ensure that the policies meet the needs of the TMO, its tenants and clients
g) agree policies which conform with equal opportunities and legal requirements

| | |
|---|---|
| What Supporting Knowledge is Needed?: | TMO's aims and objectives<br>Modular Management Agreement<br>Relevant legislation, good practice guidance and government policy<br>How policies fit into local authority structures<br>Understanding of equal opportunities issues and implications |
| NVQ Alternative: | Housing NVQ Level 4 Unit 3 |

**Development 4: Ability to Plan, Control and Negotiate Budgets**

Why Needed?:
During the development stage TMOs are responsible for submitting applications for finance and controlling their budgets. Although the TMO may delegate the responsibility for maintaining financial systems, TMO members must exercise responsibility for their budget and financial control. They must also negotiate their management and maintenance allowances

Who Needs the Ability?: At least one member of the committee should have responsibility for financial control. All committee members should have some financial awareness

What Does it Include?:
1) Contribute to the implementation of financial policies
2) Monitor and control activities against budget
3) Negotiate and agree budget with local authority

Example:
i) Treasurer takes responsibility for budget and financial control
ii) Sub-committee negotiates management and maintenance allowances (with professional support)

What Will be Assessed?: The agency will assess whether committee members:
a) assess information on costs and resources
b) obtain value for money
c) take appropriate action, with a minimum of delay, where a budget is likely to underspend or overspend
d) seek information on management and maintenance allowances
e) conduct negotiations with the council in a professional and appropriate matter, using professional assistance if necessary

What Supporting Knowledge is Needed?:
Role and responsibility of treasurer
Role of auditor
TMO's financial standing orders
Local authority housing finance
Section 16 financial monitoring requirements
TMO's management and maintenance allowance methodology
Effective negotiation

NVQ Alternative: Housing NVQ Level 3 Unit 7.3 and 7.5

| **Development 5: Ability to Present Information—Written and Spoken** | | |
|---|---|---|
| | Why Needed?: | The TMO needs to communicate its aims, policies and services. While much of the day-to-day communication may be carried out by the agency (or by the TMO staff), at least some committee members should be able to present information themselves |
| | Who Needs the Ability?: | At least one and preferably several committee members (spoken and written abilities may be held by different people) |
| | What Does it Include?: | Organising and presenting information |
| | Example: | Contributing to newsletters, speaking at a public meeting, writing letters to the council |
| | What Will be Assessed?: | The agency will assess whether the individual:<br>a) presents the information in a style that is suitable for the audience<br>b) ensures that the information is accurate and complete<br>c) structures the information clearly (beginning, middle and end)<br>d) reviews their performance |
| | What Supporting Knowledge is Needed?: | Different styles of written information<br>Effective public speaking<br>Awareness of equal opportunities issues |
| | NVQ Alternative: | Housing NVQ Level 2 Unit 3.3 |

**Development 6: Ability to Establish and Maintain Working Relationships with Other Organisations**

| | |
|---|---|
| Why Needed?: | The TMO needs to work with the local authority and other local agencies. The ability to develop relationships which assist in meeting the TMO's aims is essential |
| Who Needs the Ability?: | At least one committee member, preferably several |
| What Does it Include?: | 1) Identify and contact other organisations<br>2) Develop working relationships<br>3) Deal with conflict<br>4) Assess relationships |
| Example: | Committee members work to establish good relationships with local authority staff and councillors.<br>Committee members identify and contact a range of local organisations |
| What Will be Assessed?: | The agency will assess whether committee members:<br>a) identify organisations with which the TMO needs a working relationship<br>b) take opportunities to establish and maintain contact with these organisations<br>c) take time to develop constructive working relationships with individuals in these organisations<br>d) deal with differences of opinion and breakdowns in relationships with other organisations in an appropriate way<br>e) assess how well relationships with other organisations are working<br>f) pass suggestions for improving relationships to the appropriate people |
| What Supporting Knowledge is Needed?: | TMO's aims and objectives<br>Awareness of roles of other organisations<br>Equal opportunities<br>Effective communication |
| NVQ Alternative: | Housing NVQ Level 4 Unit 9 |

| **Development 7: Ability to Negotiate and Monitor Housing Services** | | |
|---|---|---|
| | Why Needed?: | Ability to monitor the performance of the TMO is essential. Performance standards must be re-negotiated with the local authority annually |
| | Who Needs the Ability?: | At least one member of the committee, and preferably several, should have the ability to negotiate. All committee members should be able to interpret performance monitoring reports |
| | What Does it Include?: | 1) Set objectives<br>2) Negotiate agreements<br>3) Interpret performance data<br>4) Review performance |
| | Example: | Committee members negotiate monitoring arrangements with the local authority (with professional support) |
| | What Will be Assessed?: | The agency will assess whether committee members can:<br>a) set objectives for housing functions in line with the management agreement, equal opportunities and other legal requirements<br>b) define the areas that need to be monitored and the information which will be required<br>c) negotiate appropriate arrangements for monitoring and performance measures with the local authority<br>d) conduct negotiations with the local authority in a professional and appropriate manner<br>e) interpret simple tables and graphs which show housing performance information<br>f) suggest appropriate course of action which could be taken if objectives are not achieved |
| | What Supporting Knowledge is Needed?: | TMO's aims and objectives<br>TMO's policies and standing orders<br>Management agreement<br>Equal opportunities issues and implications<br>Relevant legislation, codes of practice and government policy<br>Effective negotiation<br>Interpretation of data<br>Local authority performance standards<br>Good practice standards |
| | NVQ Alternative: | Housing NVQ Level 4 Unit 6 |

# Appendix 6  Optional Development Competences

01    Ability to select and manage staff

02    Ability to manage service contracts

03    Ability to control budgets and finance

04    Ability to provide information for customers

05    Ability to communicate housing policies, programmes and services

06    Ability to let properties

07    Ability to organise repairs and maintenance

08    Ability to plan, organise and evaluate work

**Option 1: Ability to Select and Manage Staff**

Why Needed?: This competence is a requirement for all TMOs which intend to employ staff. If staff are not appointed when competence is assessed, parts of the ability may be assessed from role-play. Committee members may use professional assistance

Who Needs the Ability?: Members of recruitment panel. Committee members who will have the responsibility for managing staff

What Does it Include?:
1) Agree staffing levels
2) Draw up selection procedure
3) Interview candidates
4) Draw up policies for staff supervision

Example: Staffing sub-committee draws up job descriptions, recruitment procedure and policies for staff supervision

What Will be Assessed?: The agency will assess whether committee members can:
a) draw up a staffing structure and job descriptions which are in line with chosen management options and within budget
b) take into account the advice of local authority and agency
c) base suggestions for selection procedure on equal opportunities and other legal requirements
d) identify the key skills, knowledge and abilities being sought
e) draw up policies for staff supervision in line with good employment practice
f) suggest ways of ensuring a healthy and safe working environment

What Supporting Knowledge is Needed?: TMO's performance standards for service delivery
Responsibilities of TMO under management agreement
Equal opportunities issues in employment
Legislative background/where to get specialist advice
Good practice in employment

NVQ Alternative: Housing NVQ Level 3 Unit B1

**Option 2: Ability to Manage Service Contracts**

| | |
|---|---|
| Why Needed?: | Contract management is a crucial element of successful housing management. This competence is needed where the TMO committee intends to carry out the task of contract negotiation, management and administration itself (rather than delegate to staff) or where day-to-day management will be carried out by an agent |
| Who Needs the Ability?: | At least one committee member, preferably several, who will be involved in contract management |
| What Does it Include?: | 1) Agree specifications for contracts to be managed by the TMO<br>2) Draw up a system for assessing tenders against contract specifications<br>3) Develop a monitoring system |
| Example: | TMO sub-committee draws up contract specification (with professional advice) and agrees contract monitoring procedure |
| What Will be Assessed?: | The agency will assess whether committee members:<br>a) suggest contract specifications in line with chosen management options and agreed service standards<br>b) take legal and equal opportunities obligations into account<br>c) ensure that service delivery targets can be met within budget<br>d) draw up monitoring procedure in line with the TMO constitution and management agreement |
| What Supporting Knowledge is Needed?: | TMO's management agreement<br>Principles of contract law<br>Methods of costing and pricing contracts<br>Tendering procedures<br>Service assessment and monitoring<br>Where to go for advice |
| NVQ Alternative: | Housing NVQ Level 4 Unit 3 |

**Option 3: Ability to Control Budgets and Finance**

Why Needed?: During the development stage TMOs are responsible for submitting applications for finance and controlling their budgets. In practice, many TMOs may delegate the responsibility for the maintenance of financial systems to staff. However, where the TMO chooses to administer financial systems itself — and intends to do so when the TMO is established — then its committee must be able to demonstrate financial competence

Who Needs the Ability?: At least one member of the committee, preferably several

What Does it Include?:
1) Make applications for funding
2) Maintain financial systems
3) Implement financial policies
4) Control activities against budget
5) Review the effectiveness of financial system

Example: The TMO member (probably the Treasurer) controls the budget and maintains financial systems

What Will be Assessed?: The agency will assess whether committee members:
a) present clear and concise applications for funding
b) support estimates of costs with valid and relevant information
c) take possible future variations in activity into account
d) are able to give further explanations if proposals are challenged
e) keep records of income and expenditure in accordance with TMO policies and legal requirements
f) authorise payments in accordance with TMO constitution and policies
g) ensure that expenditure is within agreed limits and is in line with TMO policies
h) submit regular, accurate and up-to-date financial statements to the TMO committee and DoE
i) review financial systems regularly
j) implement any suggestions arising from the review quickly

| | |
|---|---|
| What Supporting Knowledge is Needed?: | Role and responsibilities of Treasurer<br>Section 16 funding system<br>Good practice in financial control<br>Local authority finance<br>TMO finance<br>Accounting/book-keeping<br>Financial standing orders, policies and procedures of TMO<br>Role of auditor<br>Preparation/presentation of annual accounts<br>Petty cash/banking procedures<br>VAT/taxation |
| NVQ Alternative: | Housing NVQ Level 3 Unit 7 |

**Option 4: Ability to Provide Information for Customers**

| | |
|---|---|
| Why Needed?: | If the TMO committee members are carrying out day-to-day reception duties in the office, the TMO needs to ensure that those involved are able to respond to requests for advice and information |
| Who Needs the Ability?: | TMO committee members who will be working in the office |
| What Does it Include?: | 1) Identify what customer needs to know<br>2) Obtain information for customer<br>3) Provide information to customer |
| Example: | Committee member answers query from a tenant on how to apply for housing benefit. Committee members give advice on how to apply for housing to an applicant (during role-play or shadowing local authority staff) |
| What Will be Assessed?: | The agency will assess whether committee members:<br>a) ask questions which aim to obtain relevant information<br>b) refer customers to appropriate people if answers are not available<br>c) build contacts with organisations who can provide information<br>d) use sources of information (policy manuals, leaflets, people) effectively<br>e) give information which is accurate, and in line with legislation and TMO policies<br>f) respect information which is given in confidence<br>g) obtain and provide information in a suitable and courteous manner |
| What Supporting Knowledge is Needed?: | Relevant legislation and codes of practice<br>TMO's policies and procedures<br>Equal opportunities issues<br>Customer care issues<br>Other agencies who could provide information |
| NVQ Alternative: | Housing NVQ Level 3 Unit 1 |

**Option 5: Ability to Communicate Housing Policies, Programmes and Services**

| | |
|---|---|
| Why Needed?: | TMOs have a responsibility to distribute information and to involve residents and members. To do this, they need to establish suitable consultation methods. This competence is required if the TMO committee intends to carry out this function itself, rather than delegate the task to staff or agents |
| Who Needs the Ability?: | At least one, and preferably several committee members will need this ability |
| What Does it Include?: | 1) Identify who needs to be informed and consulted<br>2) Develop and organise suitable methods of communication<br>3) Present information on housing policies and programmes<br>4) Review communication strategy |
| Example: | A new procedure for reporting repairs would need wide promotion |
| What Will be Assessed?: | The agency will assess whether committee members:<br>a) identify all the people and organisations who need to be informed and consulted<br>b) take account of equal opportunities issues<br>c) identify the information needs of different types of people/ organisations<br>d) choose methods of communication which are suitable for each type of audience<br>e) present clear and accurate information which is in line with legislation and TMO policies<br>f) review methods and effectiveness |
| What Supporting Knowledge is Needed?: | TMO's Tenant Participation policy<br>Equal opportunities issues<br>Different methods of communication<br>Availability of specialist services (ie translation)<br>Procedures and good practice in organising meetings<br>Procedures and good practice for newsletters |
| NVQ Alternative: | Housing NVQ Level 3 Unit 3 |

| **Option 6: Ability to Let Properties** | | |
|---|---|---|
| | Why Needed?: | If TMO members intend to let properties themselves (rather than employing staff to carry out this function) they will need to show that they are competent in this area |
| | Who Needs the Ability?: | All TMO committee members who will be involved in letting properties |
| | What Does it Include?: | 1) Set up systems for letting houses<br>2) Applicants are interviewed and advised of options<br>3) Offer housing to applicants<br>4) Plan and arrange for empty properties to be repaired |
| | Example: | TMO committee members have shadowed local authority staff carrying out this function. Sub-committee has set up system for letting houses (with professional assistance) |
| | What Will be Assessed?: | The agency will assess whether committee members:<br>a) make suggestions for lettings systems which are in line with TMO policies and responsibilities<br>b) take equal opportunities issues and legislation into account<br>c) ensure that proposed system is efficient and cost effective<br>d) confirm applicants' circumstances<br>e) discuss options with applicants in a suitable manner<br>f) make an offer of housing in accordance with policies and procedures<br>g) implement tenancy acceptance procedures |
| | What Supporting Knowledge is Needed?: | TMO's aims and objectives<br>TMO's policy on allocations<br>Legal and equal opportunities requirements<br>Homelessness legislation<br>Local authority letting policies<br>How TMO letting policy interacts with local authority policy<br>Identify effective interviewing skills |
| | NVQ Alternative: | Housing NVQ Level 3 Unit 5 |

**Option 7: Ability to Organise Repairs and Maintenance**

| | |
|---|---|
| Why Needed?: | If TMO members intend to organise repairs and maintenance themselves (rather than employ staff or contract the service from an agent) they will need to show competence in this area |
| Who Needs the Ability?: | All TMO members who will be involved in organising repairs and maintenance |
| What Does it Include?: | 1) Set up systems for organising repairs<br>2) Inspect repairs<br>3) Plan and arrange for property to be repaired<br>4) Monitor progress of repairs |
| Example: | TMO committee members have shadowed local authority staff carrying out this function. Sub-committee has set up system for repairs reporting and monitoring (with professional assistance). |
| What Will be Assessed?: | The agency will assess whether committee members:<br>a) make suggestions for repairs systems which are in line with TMO's policy and responsibilities<br>b) take equal opportunities issues and legislation (especially health and safety regulations) into account<br>c) ensure that proposed system is efficient and cost effective<br>d) can carry out an accurate and comprehensive inspection of a property for repairs<br>e) give accurate information to appropriate people of repairs required<br>f) ensure that the work carried out complies with policy, legal requirements and conditions of contract and meets TMOs performance standards |
| What Supporting Knowledge is Needed?: | TMO's aims and objectives<br>Management agreement<br>TMO's policy and procedures for repairs<br>TMO's performance standards for repairs<br>TMO maintenance allowance<br>Legal and equal opportunities requirements<br>Contract supervision and monitoring<br>Health and safety requirement<br>Basic building technology |
| NVQ Alternative: | Housing NVQ Level 3 Unit 6 |

**Option 8: Ability to Plan, Organise and Evaluate Work**

| | |
|---|---|
| Why Needed?: | TMOs carrying out their own housing management functions (without staff) need to be able to plan, organise and assess their work |
| Who Needs the Ability?: | TMO committee members who intend to carry out day-to-day management responsibilities |
| What Does it Include?: | 1) Plan work activities to achieve objectives<br>2) Organise work<br>3) Assess effectiveness<br>4) Provide feedback on performance<br>5) Create and maintain effective working environments |
| Example: | TMO committee members plan and carry out a membership drive |
| What Will be Assessed?: | The agency will assess whether committee members:<br>a) plan work activities taking budget constraints into account<br>b) ensure that working methods are in line with TMO's objectives, policies and legal requirements<br>c) seek advice if TMO's policies and legal requirements appear to conflict<br>e) clearly define team and individual responsibilities<br>f) assess team and individual results against performance standards and budget<br>g) provide feedback on performance to each member in an appropriate manner<br>h) take action if TMO's priorities change<br>i) ensure that all work activities satisfy health and safety practice<br>j) pass recommendations for improving health and safety practice to the appropriate people without delay |
| What Supporting Knowledge is Needed?: | Health, safety and hygiene legislation<br>TMO's policies and procedures<br>Performance monitoring<br>Identify effective teamwork<br>Planning of work programmes |
| NVQ Alternative: | Housing NVQ Level 4 Unit 8 |

# Appendix 7   Organisational Checklist: Development

By the time that the agency submits a development report, the TMO should have chosen, negotiated and agreed its management options with the local authority. Policies and procedures should also be agreed.

The checklist includes 'core' elements, which all TMOs should have and optional elements, which will depend on the functions and responsibilities taken on. Items A to E are 'core' elements. Items F to K are optional elements

**A. TMO COMMITTEE STRUCTURE**

1. Does the TMO have a list of the names and addresses of committee members which indicates whether members are tenants or leaseholders? ☐

2. Has the committee structure (including sub-committees) been agreed? ☐

3. Is the structure in line with the TMO constitution and the responsibilities which the TMO plans to take over? ☐

4. Are the roles and responsibilities of officers (Chairperson, Treasurer and Secretary) clearly defined and available in writing? ☐

5. Has the TMO drawn up Standing Orders for committee meetings and working groups? ☐

6. Are committee meetings held regularly, in line with the TMO constitution? ☐

7. Are adequate agendas produced and sent out in advance of meetings? ☐

8. Are adequate minutes kept of committee meetings? ☐

9. Is there an adequate and written policy on training for committee members? ☐

**B. REGISTRATION**

1. Has the TMO registered as an Industrial and Provident Society, a company limited by guarantee or a company limited by shares? ☐

2. Are the Rules or Articles of Association held on file? ☐

3. Is there an up-to-date share/membership register? ☐

**C. MANAGEMENT AGREEMENT**

1. Has an equal opportunities policy, which complies with legal obligations and requirements for a TMO, been agreed? ☐

2. Have all policies and procedures relevant to the agreement been drawn up and included in the management agreement? ☐

3. Has the management agreement been negotiated and agreed with with the local authority? ☐

4. Have appropriate performance standards been agreed for the first year? ☐

**D. FINANCE**

1. Have financial policies, delegation and authorised signatories been approved by TMO committee? ☐

2. Are adequate and up-to-date records kept of invoices paid, payment advice notes, cheque stubs, bank statements and bank reconciliations? ☐

3. Are payments authorised and cheques signed according to procedures laid down? ☐

4. Are regular and adequate financial statements made to the TMO committee and general meetings? ☐

5. Are audited accounts available for inspection together with the auditor's letter to the TMO and the TMO response? ☐

6. Is there a set of banking procedures for handling money received? ☐

7. Is the TMO operating an adequate petty cash system which includes a list of payments made from petty cash? ☐

8. Have management and maintenance allowances been negotiated in line with *Calculating Allowances for TMOs*? ☐

9. Has the TMO drawn up a budget and cash-flow forecast for its first year of operation; which shows that the TMO is financially viable? ☐

10. Has the TMO registered with HM Customs & Excise for VAT? ☐

**E. TENANT INVOLVEMENT**

1. Is there a policy on tenant consultation and involvement, in line with the management agreement and legal responsibilities? ☐

2. Does the policy have specific regard to equal opportunities issues, including race, gender, sexual orientation and disability? ☐

3. Are public meetings and general meetings widely advertised? ☐

4. Are general meetings and annual general meetings held in accordance with the TMO constitution? ☐

5. Are newsletters and information to residents produced regularly and in a clear and readable style? ☐

**F. REPAIRS AND MAINTENANCE**

Will the TMO take any responsibility for housing repairs and maintenance    Yes/No

1) If yes, has the TMO established a repairs and maintenance policy which:

   a) complies with legal requirements and recognised good practice? ☐

   b) includes a list of items which the TMO will be responsible for and items which tenants will be responsible for? ☐

   c) includes reasonable target times for completion of repairs? ☐

2) Are there adequate procedures in place for:

   a) dealing with emergency and out-of-hours repairs? ☐

   b) checking a percentage of repairs when works are complete? ☐

   c) ensuring that there will be adequate information to monitor performance on repairs? ☐

   d) ensuring that the repairs are carried out within budget constraints? ☐

## G. RENT COLLECTION

Will the TMO take any responsibility for rent collection  Yes/No

1) If yes, does the TMO have policies and procedures which:

   a) offer tenants a choice of payment methods? ☐

   b) will keep weekly records of rent payments for each tenant? ☐

   c) ensure that there will be adequate information to monitor performance on rent collection? ☐

## H. RENT ARREARS

Will the TMO have any responsibility for dealing with rent arrears?  Yes/No

If yes, has the TMO established:

1) a rent arrears policy which complies with legal requirements and recognised good practice? ☐

2) standard arrears letters which comply with recognised good practice ☐

3) standard Notices Seeking Possession which comply with legal requirements? ☐

4) a procedure for counselling tenants or referring them to other relevant organisations? ☐

5) a procedure which will ensure adequate information to monitor performance on arrears? ☐

## I. ALLOCATIONS

Will the TMO have any responsibility for allocating property?  Yes/No

If yes, has the TMO established:

1) an allocation policy which complies with legal requirements and recognised good practice? ☐

2) a policy and procedures on nominations from the local authority and other organisations (if appropriate)? ☐

3) adequate procedures for dealing with void property? ☐

4) procedures to ensure equal opportunities monitoring of allocations? ☐

5) a procedure which will ensure adequate information to monitor performance on allocations? ☐

**J. CARETAKING AND CLEANING**

Will the TMO have any responsibility for caretaking and cleaning? Yes/No

If yes, has the TMO established:

1) agreed standards for caretaking and cleaning? ☐
2) equipment and cleansing material requirements? ☐
3) arrangements for grounds/garden maintenance? ☐
4) a procedure which will ensure adequate information to monitor performance on caretaking and cleaning? ☐

**K. EMPLOYMENT**

Will the TMO be directly employing any staff? Yes/No

If yes, has the TMO drawn up:

1) a staffing structure which is in line with the management budget? ☐
2) adequate job descriptions and person specifications for each member of staff? ☐
3) a contract of employment which complies with legal requirements? ☐
4) discipline and grievance procedures which comply with legal requirements and recognised good practice? ☐
5) a policy on staff training and development? ☐
6) policy and procedures for recruitment of staff, which take account of equal opportunities issues? ☐
7) policies for staff supervision, reporting and liaison? ☐
8) a procedure for equal opportunities monitoring of applicants/staff? ☐
9) procedures for dealing with PAYE and employers' National Insurance contributions? ☐

**L. CONTRACTED WORK**

Will the TMO be contracting services? Yes/No

If yes, has the TMO established:

1) contract and tendering procedures which comply with legal requirements and equal opportunities obligations? ☐
2) service specifications which support and develop the aims of the TMO? ☐
3) reporting and monitoring procedures? ☐
4) a timetable for contract renewal? ☐
5) lists of approved contractors? ☐

# Appendix 8   References

Scott, S., Clapham, D., Clark, A., Goodlad, R., Parkey, H. *Training for Tenant Management*, HMSO, 1994

Scott, S., Clark, A., Parkey, H. and Williams, M. *Learning to Manage*, HMSO, 1994

Scott, S., Clapham, D., Clark, A., Goodlad, R., Kintrea, K., Parkey, H., Rodgers, D., Williams, M. *The Guide to the Right to Manage*, HMSO, 1994

Institute of Public Finance Ltd *Calculating Allowances for TMOs*, HMSO, 1994

Rodgers, D. et al *The Modular Management Agreement for Tenant Management Organisations*, HMSO, 1994